Serial Killers Rage and Horror

8 Shocking True Crime Stories of Serial Killers and Killing Sprees

Serial Killers Anthology Vol.2

By

Jack Rosewood & Rebecca Lo

DISCLAIMER:

This serial killer anthology explores eight different cases of serial killers. It is not the intention of the author to defame or intentionally harm anyone involved. The interpretation of the events leading up to the discovery of the murders, are the opinion of the author as a result of researching these true crime killers. Any comments made about the motive and behavior of each killer is the sole opinion and responsibility of the author.

FREE BONUS!

Contents

Introduction 1

CHAPTER 1: Paul John Knowles - The Casanova Killer 4

Foster Care and Reform 5

Early Incarcerations 5

Dumped - Was This the Catalyst? 6

Cross Country Killing Spree 7

Abduction of an Officer 11

Death before Justice 13

Possibility of Others 13

'The Day She Died' 14

Beware the Attractive Charmer 16

Memories Remain 18

Knowles' Terrifying Timeline 19

CHAPTER 2: Leslie Irvin - The Mad Dog Killer 22

Burglar Gone Bad 23

Many Murders Done 23

Caught and Charged...26

Irvin on Trial...27

Prejudicial Publicity 28

Dodging the Death Penalty...................................29

The End of Mad Dog...32

No Explanations...33

Irvin's Timeline 35

CHAPTER 3: Wayne Williams - The Atlanta Child Murders...... 37

Early Years 38

Splash from a Bridge 39

Arrest and Trial for Two Kills................................41

Atlanta Child Murders...42

List of Child Victims 48

Williams is Number 1 Suspect 49

"I'm Innocent"...51

Recent Developments..54

Interview with Williams in 1991 57

The Psychological Assessment that Wasn't 59

Did He Act Alone? 61

Timeline Including Alleged Crimes 62

CHAPTER 4: The Connecticut River Valley Killer.....................**65**

Known Murders and Survivors 67

The Main Suspects 72

Other Possible Crimes...77

The Case Goes Cold...79

The Murder of Jessica Briggs 80

Survivor Boroski Identifies Nicholaou 82

CHAPTER 5: Michel Fourniret - The Ogre of the Ardennes **85**

Behind the Façade..86

Hunting for Virgins 87

Multiple Murders Committed 88

Confessions of a Wife..91

Investigation of Fourniret 94

Trial and Conviction 98

Aftermath- Personal and Public............................ 101

Who Was the True Monster? 102

Latest Updates 105

Timeline of Murder 106

CHAPTER 6: Gilbert Paul Jordan - The Boozing Barber **108**

The Beginnings of the Boozing Barber 108

Many Alleged Victims... 110

Investigation and Arrest.. 113

Conviction and Appeal 114

Other Possible Victims 116

Searching for Mary.. 116

Targeting Aboriginal Women................................... 117

A Strange Method of Murder 119

The Final Years 120

Jordan's Criminal Timeline...................................... 121

CHAPTER 7: Robert Hansen - The Butcher Baker 125

A Troubled Start in Life 125

Early Crimes... 126

Hunting His Prey... 128

The Escapee.. 133

Arrest and Plea Bargain.. 135

Finding the Dead 141

Identifying Eklutna Annie.. 148

Hansen's Final Days.. 148

Hansen's Timeline of Events................................... 150

CHAPTER 8: Steve Wright - The Suffolk Strangler **155**

The Early Days 156

A Love of Prostitutes 158

Crossing into Murder 159

The Victims 160

Operation Sumac................................ 163

The Jury Decides................................... 165

Possible Links to Other Murders 170

Controversial Media Coverage 171

Where did it All Go So Wrong?............................. 175

The Lucky Ones................................... 176

Did He Work Alone?.............................. 179

Where is He Now?................................. 180

Wright's Timeline 181

More books by Jack Rosewood................................. 183

GET THESE BOOKS FOR FREE 188

A Note From The Author........................... 189

Introduction

Fear and loathing, horror and disgust, are some of the most powerful emotions in the human world, and nothing triggers them more, than the slaughter of innocent people. For the serial killer, these emotions aren't upsetting; on the contrary, they are thrilling, exciting, and invoke a feeling of power over those they consider to be weak. They care not for the feelings of their victims or their loved ones, they are only concerned with what the act of murder will provide for them.

Eight killers, eight more stories of rage and horror. Some of these cases changed how society carried out their daily lives, and others forever altered how laws were perceived and enacted. But each story contains the details of who these killers were, and the terror they caused to the communities in which they decided to inflict such horrible fear.

Steve Wright, the Suffolk Strangler, preyed on the drug addicted prostitutes in Ipswich, England. He saw these women as something to be used as a way for him to indulge his own dreams and fantasies. They were the easy targets, the ones who wouldn't be missed straight away. Similarly, Robert Hansen chose the victims he thought were worthless, that nobody

1

would care about if they disappeared. Then he chased them through the Alaskan wilderness armed with a hunting rifle and a knife.

One of the most shocking stories of all time is that of Wayne Williams, the alleged Atlanta Child Murderer. Although only charged with the murders of two adult men, Williams has remained the number one suspect in the deaths of dozens of children in Atlanta for decades. He claims he is innocent, but forensic science disagrees. As he fights for freedom, his DNA is discovered on the bodies of at least two children...this has yet to be explained by him.

In a city in France, lived the Ogre of the Ardennes, Michel Fourniret, who had a lust for young female children. Along with his wife, he would abduct young girls, subject them to unspeakable examinations and torture, then he would kill them and toss them aside as though they were nothing. His wife cries 'foul', that she was abused, threatened, and terrified for her own life, therefore did what he asked of her. But who exactly was the real monster - Michel or his wife?

The story of the Boozing Barber is perhaps one of the most controversial serial killer cases to date. He used a murder method that had never been used before, and it was debatable at the time if there were indeed any murders at all. Something so readily available and willing participants, equals the death of a number of unfortunate women.

These are just some of the monsters that have walked among everyday societies around the globe. Their stories may upset you, they may fascinate you or they may even sicken you. Either way, by telling the stories the victims are never forgotten. For what happened to them, was no fault of their own - it was the monsters.

CHAPTER 1:
Paul John Knowles - The Casanova Killer

Knowles was nicknamed 'The Casanova Killer' by the press because of his good looks and charm, not because he was a great romantic lover. Over a very short period of time, Knowles committed at least 20 murders across the country, and later claimed to have killed 35, though this has not been corroborated by the investigators. Unlike killers that stalked their victims for the thrill of killing, most of the murders committed by Knowles seemed to be opportunistic, and there was often some kind of financial gain, especially when he needed a vehicle.

An escape artist who broke out of prison and a man who could charm anyone with a smile, Knowles appeared to be on some sort of high-octane killing spree, sparing few that he came into contact with, and showing no preference of killing women over men. It didn't matter who the victim was, if they were in his way or they had something he needed or wanted, he took their belongings as well as their lives.

Foster Care and Reform

Knowles was born on April 17, 1946, in Orlando, Florida. As a youngster, he was constantly getting into trouble with the law, predominantly for petty crimes. After one of his arrests, his father 'washed his hands of him', uninterested in trying to help or rehabilitate his son. As a result, Knowles was sent to live in foster care.

As his teenage years progressed, his petty crimes continued. Knowles eventually ended up living in reformatories, a place for young criminals that are unable to go to an adult prison. There has been a lot of research and discussion about the effects of foster care and reformatory life on young children and offenders. Although it is unknown whether this affected Knowles as an adult, there is clear documentation and studies that show foster care in particular can increase the chances of a child progressing towards violent crime.

Early Incarcerations

The first known theft committed by Knowles was when he was just seven years old, and he was picked up by the police for stealing a bicycle. He was in and out of trouble from then onwards, and in 1968, he was arrested and charged with attempted burglary. He received a three year sentence at a Florida state prison, of which he served the whole sentence.

In 1971, Knowles was released from prison, but wasn't free for very long. That same year, he was arrested again on similar burglary charges and sent back to prison. A year later, Knowles escaped from a prison work camp, and after three weeks on the run, he was recaptured. This resulted in an extension of three years being added on to his existing sentence.

While Knowles was incarcerated, he managed to get the attention of a cocktail waitress in San Francisco Angela Covic, by corresponding through letters. On their first meeting, Knowles proposed to her and she accepted. She was so enthralled by Knowles that she hired a criminal attorney, who subsequently was able to get an early release for Knowles. Out of prison in May 1974, Knowles moved to California, along with Angela Covic, and tried to make a fresh start.

Dumped - Was This the Catalyst?

The relationship didn't last however, once she saw his darker side. She had also received a warning from a psychic that a dangerous man had entered her life. So, Angela Covic ended the relationship. Knowles went back to Florida, and once again he got himself into trouble. He was arrested soon after arriving back in Florida for an aggravated assault, after stabbing a bartender during a fight. It seemed that prison couldn't keep him behind bars though, because on July 26, 1974, Knowles picked the lock on his cell and escaped again.

Knowles later claimed to have killed three people on the night

Angela Covic ended their relationship, but this has never been verified. Until the relationship ended, although a criminal, Knowles had not committed any serious violent crimes. Perhaps it was the end of the relationship that spurred him on to commit the many murders that followed.

Cross Country Killing Spree

The night Knowles broke out of his cell, July 26, 1974, was the first night of what would become his cross county killing spree. On that night, he broke into the home of an elderly woman, Alice Curtis, looking for money and valuables to steal. He tied 65 year old Alice up and gagged her while he ransacked her home. Tragically, Alice choked to death on her dentures, and Knowles has never said whether she died while he was still in the home or after he had left.

Knowles stole Alice's car, a Dodge Dart, to make his getaway. He was connected to the crime very quickly, and knowing that he had been advertised as a wanted fugitive, Knowles had to get rid of the car. He picked a street to abandon the vehicle on, and it was there that he saw two people he recognized - Lillian and Mylette Anderson, who were acquaintances of the Knowles family. Worried that they would identify him, he kidnapped the two young girls. Lillian was eleven years old and Mylette was seven, Knowles strangled both girls and buried their remains in a swamp nearby.

Soon after killing the two girls, Knowles picked up a teenager who was hitchhiking. She turned out to be Ima Jean Sanders, 13, although it took decades to identify her. She had run away from Beaumont in Texas, and disappeared from Georgia on August 1, 1974. Knowles admitted killing the young teenager, but was never able to give a reason.

Knowles met Marjorie Howie, 49, in Atlantic Beach, Florida on August 2, 1974. It's uncertain whether she invited him back to her apartment or if he forced her, but either way, Knowles strangled her with a nylon stocking. He then stole her television, and it is believed he later gave it to a former girlfriend.

Towards the end of August, Knowles had moved on to Musella, Georgia. There, he went to the home of Kathie Sue Pierce and forced his way inside. Kathie was at home with her three year old son at the time. Knowles took her into the bathroom and strangled her with a telephone cord he had cut. After he had killed her, he left, without physically hurting the little boy.

Knowles was in Lima, Ohio, on September 3, 1974, and went into a pub called Scott's Inn. There he met an account executive for Ohio Power Company, William Bates, aged 32. The bartender later recalled seeing Bates having drinks with a redheaded man before the two men left the bar together. Bates was a married man, and after his wife reported him missing, police went back to the bar and found the Dodge Dart that had belonged to Alice Curtis, the first victim, and the car belonging to Bates was missing. The nude body of Bates was later found in October, in woods nearby, and he had been strangled to death.

Knowles had of course taken Bates' car, and traveled on to a camping ground in Ely, Nevada. On September 18, Knowles attacked two elderly campers, Emmett and Lois Johnson. Both were bound before being shot to death. At the time, authorities thought it was a random murder, particularly because they had been killed in a different manner to the other victims. Despite Knowles using their credit cards for a while after he killed them, police had no clue he was responsible until his confession.

Knowles continued his killing spree on September 21, and by now he was in Seguin, Texas. Charlynn Hicks, his next victim, was stranded on the side of the road after her motorcycle broke down. Knowles abducted Charlynn and raped her, eventually strangling her to death with her own pantyhose. He then dragged her body through a barbed-wire fence where it was found four days later.

The next town Knowles terrorized was Birmingham, Alabama. He met Ann Dawson, a beautician, on September 23, and it is uncertain whether she went with him willingly or he abducted her. Either way, the two traveled together with Ann paying all the expenses until September 29. On that day, Knowles killed Ann and disposed of her body in the Mississippi River. However, her remains were never found.

Knowles entered the home of Karen Wine and her 16 year old

daughter Dawn, in Marlborough, Connecticut on the night of October 16. He tied up both women, raped them, and then strangled them to death with a nylon stocking. The only item police could identify as being missing from the home was a tape recorder.

On October 18, Knowles broke into the home of Doris Hosey, 53, in Woodford, Virginia. He shot Doris to death with a rifle belonging to her husband, then after wiping his prints off, he left the gun next to her lifeless body. When police investigated the murder, they couldn't find any signs to indicate the motive was robbery, so they were at a loss as to why Doris was killed and by whom.

By this time, Knowles was still driving around in the car that had belonged to Bates. He was now in Key West, Florida, and had just picked up two hitchhikers when he was stopped by a police officer for a traffic violation. The officer had no idea who Knowles was, and that he was a wanted man, and he let him go. The event shook Knowles so much that he let his two captives go unharmed, dropping them off in Miami. Knowles contacted his lawyer, who suggested he surrender to the authorities, but he refused. Instead he met with his lawyer and handed him a tape with his confession on it. He then fled.

Knowles moved on to Milledgeville, Georgia, and on November 6, he befriended Carswell Carr, and was invited back to Carswell's home for drinks and to spend the night. During the evening Knowles stabbed Carswell to death, then strangled his teenage daughter. He attempted to engage in necrophilia with the corpse of the 15 year old girl, but he was unsuccessful.

On November 8, Knowles was in Atlanta, and met Sandy Fawkes, a British journalist while he was drinking at a bar. Over the next couple of days, they spent time together, but Sandy claimed Knowles was unable to perform sexually despite numerous attempts. They parted on November 10, but the following day, Knowles picked up a friend of Sandy's called Susan MacKenzie, and demanded sex while pointing a gun at her. She managed to get away and informed the police immediately, but when the police tried to capture him, he waved a sawed-off shotgun at them and managed to escape.

Knowles next appeared in West Palm Beach, Florida, at which time he broke into the home of Beverly Mabee, an invalid, and kidnapped her sister. Stealing their car, he traveled to Fort Pierce in Florida, and unusually, he released his hostage without harming her. Both women had managed to escape the terrible fate that so many before them had suffered.

Abduction of an Officer

The car Knowles had stolen was spotted on November 17, by Highway Patrol Trooper Charles Eugene Campbell. The trooper ordered Knowles to pull over near Perry, Florida, but during the attempted arrest, a violent struggle between the two men took place. Knowles managed to grab hold of the trooper's pistol, and taking him hostage, Knowles drove off in the patrol car. He came across a motorist, James Meyer, and used the police siren to pull him over so he could switch vehicles.

Now Knowles had two hostages, and he couldn't (or wouldn't) let either of them live to give evidence against him. So, he took both of them into a wooded area in Pulaski County, Georgia. He handcuffed them to a tree then executed them by a shot to the head. Police had now set up a road block in Henry County, Georgia, which Knowles tried to crash through but he lost control, crashing the car into a tree.

Knowles took off on foot, firing at the officers chasing him as he ran. The chase involved police dogs, helicopters and law enforcement officers from multiple agencies. Yet his escape finally came to an end when he was cornered by a civilian who held him at gunpoint with a shotgun, several miles away from where the main search was being conducted. The civilian forced Knowles to a home nearby and the police were notified.

If the civilian hadn't come across Knowles, he would most likely have escaped, as his location was far away from where the police thought he was. Once the authorities had Knowles in custody, he quickly confessed to committing 35 murders, but they were only ever able to corroborate 20 of them.

Death before Justice

While in custody, Knowles claimed he had dumped the pistol he had taken from Trooper Campbell and shot him with, in Henry County, Georgia. On December 18, 1974, Knowles was being escorted to the location by Sheriff Earl Lee and Georgia Bureau of Investigation Agent Ronnie Angel. As they travelled down Interstate 20, with Knowles handcuffed in the back seat, he somehow managed to grab hold of Lee's handgun, firing it through the holster during the process. While Knowles struggled with Lee over the gun, Agent Angel fired three times into Knowles' chest, and he died instantly.

Possibility of Others

Two other hitchhikers were last seen on November 2, 1974, and there is speculation that Knowles was responsible for their murders. Edward Hilliard and Debbie Griffin were hitchhiking near Milledgeville, Georgia, when they were killed. The body of Hilliard was found in woods nearby, but the remains of Griffin have never been found. Knowles was strongly suspected of committing these murders because he was known to be in the location at the time and it fit with other murders he had committed of hitchhikers.

Unfortunately, the taped confession Knowles had given his lawyer before his capture was damaged, and not all of the information he gave could be heard. However, a hand-written summary was able to be created. Knowles had claimed he killed 35, but the authorities initially thought that figure was closer to 18, before they took into account the murders of Hilliard and Griffin, which increased the total to 20.

However, there is likely to be more victims of Knowles out there somewhere. A link was discovered between Knowles and the skeletal remains of a woman by the Georgia Bureau of Investigation. The young woman had gone missing in 1974, during Knowles' killing spree, from Warner-Robins, Georgia. Knowles was known to have been in the area at the time. Using the hand written summary of the tape recording, the authorities are convinced this victim was indeed one of Knowles'.

'The Day She Died'

In 2011, the family members of Ima Jean Sanders, the 13 year old girl who had been murdered 37 years prior, were summoned to a conference room at the Texas police department. It was then that they were informed officially that Ima had been a victim of Knowles during his killing spree. Although her remains had been found in April 1976, it had taken this long to match them with Ima.

The remains of the young victim were kept in a box at the Georgia state crime lab for 35 years. All that time, they were simply labelled as 'unidentified victim No. 5'. She was thought to have been a victim of Knowles, but until they could identify her, nothing was certain. Thankfully, the family of Ima Sanders had never given up on finding her, and they had continued to push for information all these years.

The identification was eventually made possible using DNA samples from one of Ima's sisters and her mother, Betty Wisecup. One of her sisters, Sharon Chessher, had only been four years old when Ima disappeared. On the last day Sharon ever saw Ima, the older girl had told Sharon to go inside their mobile home and lock the doors, as she left with some friends.

It's believed that she had been hitchhiking when Knowles picked her up, and he raped and strangled her to death in the woods. A letter written by US Attorney Ronald T. Knight in 1975 which is believed to be related to Ima's death was given to the authorities, and part of the letter read:

"Sometime in August, 1974, Knowles picked up a white, female hitchhiker named Alma who represented her age as 13 or 14 but who appeared to be in her late teens. He carried this girl to a wooded area some distance from Macon, possibly west. He raped her and then strangled her and left her body in the woods between trees.

"Approximately two weeks later, he returned to the location and found that the body had been moved eight or 10 feet away apparently by animals. The body was greatly deteriorated and barely identifiable as a human being. Knowles found her jawbone and buried it in the area."

Knowles was always a suspect in the killing of the girl because of the transcript of one of his audio 'confession' tapes. He had discussed raping and strangling a young girl he picked up hitchhiking, and had said her name as 'Alma' in August 1974. After the murder, he disposed of her remains somewhere near Macon.

Betty stated, "It was hard to know what happened, but it was good to know. I always had a feeling she'd eventually come home."

For a long time authorities hadn't even considered Ima was the body in the box because her original missing person's report had become lost over the years.

Beware the Attractive Charmer

Many who came into contact with Knowles described him as an attractive man, with long red hair, slight stubble on his face, and a cigarette often dangling from his mouth, which at the time was considered 'sexy'. But not only did he look like a combination of Robert Redford and Ryan O'Neal, the heartthrobs of the generation, he also had a personality to match.

Knowles was a charmer, one who could easily persuade women in particular. His former partner, Sandy Fawkes, described him as being the type of man who would drape a coat over your shoulders if you looked cold, or would rush to your aid if he thought you were injured. However, by the same token, the gifts he showered on her were the ill-gotten gains from some of his murder victims.

There is a false belief that serial killers are uneducated or not 'cultured' enough to indulge in normal pleasures such as reading a book. Knowles though, was very fond of reading, and one of his favorite books was 'Jonathan Livingston Seagull by Richard Bach. The story is of a bored bird who wants to be free, and perhaps Knowles saw something of himself in the character. He also favoured books about people he considered outlaws, such as Bonnie and Clyde, John Dillinger and Babyface Nelson. He apparently stated in his youth that his goal was to become an outlaw, hoping to one day become famous for being bad.

Regarding Knowles' confessions of killing 35 people, it is common for killers to exaggerate their figures to make themselves look even more evil, besides, if they are going to get life or death for one murder, they may as well add a few more to the list. Because the primary goal for Knowles was to be famous, it is highly possible that the true figure was the 20 that police have linked him to and he simply wanted to ensure his fame was grand.

Throughout his short-lived imprisonment while awaiting a trial, Knowles never showed any signs of guilt or remorse for the murders. He described them without any other emotion other than pride. He loved all the attention he was getting. It's a shame he was killed before any psychological assessment could be done, as it would have been interesting to see what the diagnosis would have been.

Memories Remain

For those police officers and investigators who worked the case of Knowles, the memories of the man and the atrocious murders he committed remain in their minds. According to Officer Jimmy Josey of Milledgeville police, there was no motive given by Knowles for the murders.

"He had no compunction about killing you, makes no difference whether he strangled you, whether he shot you, whether he stabbed you or what," Josey stated. "He was a martial arts expert. He was tough. He was mean."

Former Special Agent Roy Harris of the Georgia Bureau of Investigation recalled what it was like the day they investigated the murders of Carswell Carr and his teenage daughter Mandy.

"They took me into where Mr. Carr was first, in his bedroom, and that was bad enough. But then they took me back to Mandy's room in the back part of the house, who was 15 years old. Seeing a child like that is just awful. It's something I remember to this day."

According to Josey, "Knowles knew what he was, what he had done and where he was going. He made the statement even though we fingerprinted and photographed him and his exact words were, 'they're going to smoke me before this is over '.'"

Following his arrest, a trooper and Josey took him to the County Jail, and at that stage, they still hadn't located Trooper Charles

Campbell, whom Knowles had taken hostage. The trooper said to Knowles, "For humanitarian and Christian ground, tell me where my trooper is."

Knowles smirked and replied, "You know I can't tell you that."

The Casanova Killer, Paul John Knowles, is buried in the Jacksonville Memory Gardens, Clay County, Florida.

Knowles' Terrifying Timeline

April 17, 1946

Paul John Knowles is born.

July 26, 1974

Knowles picked a lock in his cell in jail and escaped. The same day he broke into the home of Alice Curtis and robbed her, and she choked to death on her dentures. Picked up Lillian and Mylette Anderson and murdered them.

August 1, 1974

Picked up 13 year old hitchhiker Ima Jean Sanders and killed her.

August 2, 1974

Murdered Marjorie Howie in Atlantic Beach, Florida.

End of August

Murdered Kathie Sue Pierce in Musella, Georgia.

September 3, 1974

Met William Bates at a bar in Lima, Ohio, and murdered him and took his car.

September 18, 1974

Shot and killed two elderly campers, Emmett and Lois Johnson, in Ely, Nevada.

September 21, 1974

Picked up Charlynn Hicks after her car broke down in Seguin, Texas, and murdered her.

September 29, 1974

Murdered Ann Dawson in Birmingham, Alabama.

October 16, 1974

Broke into the home of Karen Wine and her teenage daughter, in Marlborough, Connecticut. Both were raped and murdered.

October 18, 1974

Broke into the home of Doris Hosey and shot her to death, in Woodford, Virginia.

November 2, 1974

Two hitchhikers murdered, Edward Hilliard and Debbie Griffin.

November 6, 1974

Met Carswell Carr in Milledgeville, Georgia, and was invited back to his house for a drink. Murdered both Carswell and his teenage daughter.

November 17, 1974

Abducted and murdered Florida State Trooper Charles Eugene Campbell, and civilian James Meyer in Florida. Knowles captured by a civilian and arrested by the police.

December 18, 1974

While traveling in a vehicle with police officers, a scuffle broke out and Knowles was shot and killed.

CHAPTER 2:
Leslie Irvin - The Mad Dog Killer

Irvin went on a killing spree that lasted four months from December 1954, and by the end of it, six people were dead. The counties of Vanderburgh and Posey in Indiana and Henderson in Kentucky were living in fear, with nobody knowing who or where the next victim would be killed.

In each case, robbery and burglary were the main motive. But, Irvin had committed lots of burglaries before and hadn't harmed anyone, so why did his modus operandi change? He had already spent nine years of a sentence behind bars, and perhaps he wanted to make sure nobody could identify him in any future crimes.

Irvin was given the nickname 'Mad Dog' during his court appearance where he entered on all fours, tied to a leash, and barking like a dog. But Irvin was far from mad...it was all just a ploy to try and swing the juror's favor, but instead made him look like a fool.

Burglar Gone Bad

Before Irvin became a killer, he had quite a prolific criminal history, most notably for burglary and armed robbery. In 1945, he was sentenced to serve 10 to 20 years for an armed robbery in Indianapolis, of which he completed nine years before being released. It was then, May 1954, that Irvin moved to Evansville, and by December that year, his crimes had taken on a more violent method.

Many Murders Done

Irvin went on a terrifying murder spree that would last five months, and leave six people dead. His first victim was Mary Holland, 33, a woman who was three months pregnant at the time. On December 2, 1954, Mary's husband Doc found his wife slumped behind the toilet in the Bellemeade Liquor Store. Her father owned the store, and Mary took turns with him running it. She had been at the store since 5:30pm, and just after 11:00pm, Doc went to the store to help her close for the night.

As soon as Doc entered the store, he could tell that something wasn't right with the scene. Mary's purse was lying on the floor, open, and her billfold was missing. There was also a bottle of whiskey left open on the counter, and when he called out to her, she didn't answer. When he discovered Mary, she had been shot in the temple at close range, and there were a few cuts and bruises on her body that likely happened as she fell behind the toilet.

According to Doc, the murderer likely managed to get away with approximately $250, which was a considerable sum in those days. He knew that Mary would have just handed over the money if asked for it, as they had a policy to do so if they faced a robbery. So in his mind, there had been no reason to so ruthlessly murder Mary and her unborn child.

Three weeks later, on December 22, the next brutal killing occurred. Wesley Kerr spoke to his wife on the phone during his late shift at the Standard Oil Station. He had taken a quick break to talk to his wife Peggy to finalize their Christmas holiday plans. A military veteran, Kerr had managed to survive both World War II and the Korean War, and afterwards he had married Peggy and they had moved to Evansville in 1953.

At some point between 1:30am and 1:45 am, Kerr had been shot in the back of the head and the cash register was emptied of just a few dollars. When police arrived on the scene to investigate, they found Kerr's body in the bathroom. He had only been working in the job for a few months and left behind Peggy and three young children.

On March 21, 1955, the 7 year old son of Wilhelmina Sailer returned home from school and found his mother lying face down on the living room floor. She had been shot once in the head. A few minutes after the discovery, her husband John arrived home. He found Wilhelmina's purse lying on their bed, open and empty. Because she only ever carried small amounts of cash, the killer likely got away with very little money at all.

At first the authorities couldn't see a link between the murder of Wesley Kerr, Mary Holland and Wilhelmina Sailer, largely because of the distance between the crime scenes. However, they did agree that the same type of weapon had been used in all three murders.

On the morning of March 27, 1955, police were called to investigate the discovery of two bodies found lying in stagnant water beside a rural road. Both men had been shot in the head, after their hands were tied behind their backs with their own belts. They were quickly identified as Goebel and Raymond Duncan. Sheriff Lee Williams and Deputy Cleo Gish were tasked with the job of notifying the next of kin, but when they arrived at the family home, they made a gruesome discovery.

On entering the home, they found the body of Elizabeth Duncan sprawled on the bed, having been shot to death. Beside the body was her 3 year old daughter, who informed the officers that her 'mommy' was asleep. They heard a moaning noise coming from another room and rushed to investigate. Inside they found Mamie Duncan, the matriarch of the family, and although she had been shot in the head she was still alive. Mamie was left permanently blind and any memory she may have had of the incident was erased by the physical trauma.

Caught and Charged

The authorities were at a loss as to who was committing these atrocious, cold-blooded murders, but they did have one lead - a car that had been seen in the area just days before the murders of the Duncan family. It had been reported as a suspicious vehicle, an old Chevy with a dent in the front. It wasn't much of a lead, until a group of boys in Vanderburgh County decided to try and catch the killer.

Gary Peerman, his brothers and some friends were all searching the backroads of the County, all jammed into a 1940 Ford, and determined to find the mystery man who was terrorizing the area. In late March, just before the Duncan killings, they noticed a man parked on a gravel road near the home where Peerman lived. The man was urinating in the woods on the side of the road, when Gary called out, "Bud what the hell are you doing? We're investigators!"

As he yelled out the joke to the stranger, he had no idea that it was the very man they were hunting for. He wrote down the license plate of the man's vehicle, and after the description of the car seen near the Duncan home was broadcast, they notified the police. It seemed to be the same car. Authorities acted quickly, and identified the owner of the car from the license plate and tracked him down at work.

Police went to the SIGECO power plant in Yankeetown and confronted Leslie Irvin on April 8, 1955. He had soot all over his

26

face when he was arrested and placed in the Gibson County Jail, which was considered to be 'escape-proof'. He was fairly quickly charged with the six murders. According to the investigators, Irvin also confessed to committing 24 burglaries and robberies in four counties. When they searched Irvin, they found in his possession the wallet of Wesley Kerr.

Irvin on Trial

Before Irvin could go on trial, the decision had to be made whether he would go to court in Indiana or Kentucky first, as he had committed murders in both states. Indiana won out, and the trial was set to take place in Vanderburgh County. However, the attorney appointed to defend Irvin immediately requested a change of venue, because it would be difficult to find a jury who would be impartial in their judgment. The request was successful, but the trial was only moved a short distance away, to Gibson County. As the beginning processes of the trial got underway, the attorney continued to move for a further change in venue, because of the media coverage in the area. Two more motions were put forward, but were denied.

The attorney then filed eight motions for continuances to delay the trial, and these were also denied. When it came to jury selection, 268 out of the potential 430 jurors were excused, because their opinions of Irvin's guilt were firm. A further 103 were excused because they were opposed to the death penalty. By the time the jury selection was finalized, eight of the twelve selected were convinced Irvin was a guilty man.

Irvin's nickname 'Mad Dog' initially came about because of the manner in which he was brought into the courtroom each day, attached to what looked very much like a chain dog lead. The brutal nature of the murders he committed contributed to the nickname, and in the prosecutor's closing statement, he referred to Irvin as 'Mad Dog'. The jury agreed with both the description of Irvin and his crimes, and he was sentenced to death.

Prejudicial Publicity

The 6th Amendment constitutional claim arose because of the intensive media coverage that occurred in the locations of the murders and the trial. The six murders had all occurred in Evansville, Indiana, The news broadcasts and newspaper articles about the crimes caused an immense amount of both excitement and horror throughout Evansville, in nearby Vanderburgh County, and in Gibson County.

Not long after Irvin was arrested, in April 1955, the local police officials along with the County Prosecutor issued statements to the press, which were then heavily publicized. These press releases all stated that Irvin had confessed to killing the six victims, so in the mind of the public, he was naturally guilty. The defence team therefore sought two changes of venue, of which only one is permitted in Indiana due to the local statute, to ensure a fair trial would take place.

This case was the first time in Indiana that there had been a clear conflict between the media coverage and subsequent effect on the opinions of the local public and the defendant's right to a fair trial free from prejudice.

Dodging the Death Penalty

The first date of execution given to Irvin was to occur on June 12, 1956. At that time he was confined in what was considered to be an escape-proof facility in Princeton, Indiana. In January of that year, he was scheduled to be transferred to the Indiana State Prison, located in Michigan City. However, Irvin had decided that not only was he not going to move to the new prison, he was also going to do whatever he could to dodge the death chamber.

On January 21, Irvin made his move. He somehow managed to get through three locked doors, and escaped into the night. For days, the news of his escape dominated the front pages of the local newspapers, and the police posted guards outside the homes of key people from the trial. These included the Prosecutor, Paul Weaver, Howard Sandusky, the assistant prosecutor, and Chief of Detectives Dan Hudson. A 24 hour guard was also posted outside the home of Irvin's mother.

Following his escape, Irvin traveled to Las Vegas, then on to Los Angeles, and finally ended up in San Francisco. His freedom was to be short-lived however, and he was arrested on February 9.

The circumstances of his arrest were quite remarkable, considering the arresting officers had no idea who Irvin was, let alone that he was a wanted fugitive. They had arrested him in a pawnshop, and upon his apprehension he informed them of the following:

"I'm Leslie Irvin and I'm wanted in Indiana for six murders. I've been convicted of one and I'm not guilty of any."

Indiana State Police Lt. Willard Walls, along with Detective Sgt. W. W. Cornett and Gibson County Sheriff Earl Hollen, arrived in San Francisco on the evening of Friday, February 11, to collect Irvin and return him to Indiana. They didn't expect Irvin to try and fight the extradition, but that is exactly what he did.

Irvin appeared before the San Francisco Municipal Court to be arraigned on the fugitive charge, and managed to secure a continuance so he could have time to talk to his attorneys. At that time, he was informed by his attorneys that there had been a delay in their motion for a new trial.

Eventually Irvin's bid to fight the extradition back to Indiana failed, and the authorities soon learned it wasn't going to be easy to extradite Irvin. Twice they had to abort plans to fly Irvin to Indiana because of journalists finding out the flight times and swarming the airport to report on the serial killer's departure. Therefore, they decided to send him back via train. On February 15, Irvin boarded a train to Chicago, handcuffed and with a chain leash attached to the cuffs.

When Irvin arrived in Chicago, he and the accompanying officers were met by what can only be described as a police convoy, consisting of three cars carrying officers. He was taken immediately to the Indiana State Prison in Michigan City, the same prison he was meant to be transferring to before his daring escape. What ensued were numerous court appearances, legal motions, and arguments, until the Indiana Supreme Court granted Irvin a stay of execution until the beginning of December, 1956.

His attorneys presented a 5,000 page trial transcript to the state Supreme Court, arguing the extreme prejudice and bias that occurred during Irvin's trial that had resulted in the death penalty. His execution was stayed further, until March 29, 1957, and then until July 9, the same year. On the same day that his last stay was due to expire, the U.S. Circuit Court of Appeals granted an indefinite stay of execution, just five hours before Irvin was scheduled to be executed.

The Supreme Court eventually decided on June 5, 1961, that Irvin was entitled to a new trial, based on the pretrial publicity that had prevented him from having a fair trial. This was a landmark decision, because it forever changed the way information about criminal cases could be published by the media, and how the authorities went about releasing any information.

At the end of the new trial, June 13, 1962, the jury once again found Irvin guilty of first-degree murder for the killing of Wesley Kerr. They had deliberated for just over five hours before reaching their decision. This time, Irvin was sentenced to life imprisonment.

One question many asked of Irvin was how he had managed to escape that cold night in January, 1956. Irvin explained to reporter Joe Aaron that he had made at least 50 keys, using the covers from paperback novels, which he then covered in glue and tinfoil. By trying them all out in the locks, he discovered he had managed to make two keys that would open the doors successfully.

The End of Mad Dog

Irvin remained incarcerated at the Michigan State Prison for the rest of his living days. During his imprisonment, Irvin developed a remarkable skill for working with leather. He spent his days crafting purses, belts and billfolds, among other items, and these were then sold in the prison store. Many inmates develop skills that are more creative while they are in prison, particularly painting, and there has been a lot of controversy about the sales of the items they create. It is unknown whether Irvin received the proceeds from his handiwork or whether they went elsewhere.

Throughout his time before the courts, Irvin had managed to avoid four dates with the electric chair, but his life behind bars wasn't to be a particularly long one. Irvin developed lung cancer, and on November 9, 1983, he died at the age of 59 years.

No Explanations

For those who grew up with or lived near Irvin, nobody could have suspected that he would go on to become a serial killer. They described him as a really nice person, always polite, and even some reporters who worked on his case referred to him as personable. He had an uncanny ability to leave a good impression on those he came into contact with. Somewhat ironically, before he was arrested Irvin used to often visit a local bar and drink beer with police officers when they were off-duty. Even they suspected nothing.

His former parole officer also had no idea that Irvin was even capable of committing a murder, let alone six. He used to report in at the parole officers house, and on some occasions even stayed for dinner, he was just such a nice person, or so it seemed.

An intelligent man with a high level of knowledge about baseball, Irvin had an air of genuine friendliness about him. Even when he committed burglaries before the murders he used to leave 30 cents behind so that the victim would not be left with nothing.

Once he was incarcerated, Irvin was considered a model inmate, and was described as being one of the cleanest prisoners they had in Gibson County. He was always clean and tidy, and never had to be told to shower or clean himself up.

So how is it possible that this kind, friendly, genuine nice guy, was capable of killing so many innocent people? Charles Griffo, a journalist with the Indianapolis Star, was given the opportunity to interview Irvin to try and understand that very question. He also interviewed those who thought they knew Irvin well - his family, neighbors and old school mates. When Irvin was at school, they claimed he tended to get upset easily especially if the teacher punished him. He also despised being called Leslie, to him it was a girl's name, and he tried to get everyone to call him either Bud or Les.

His family reported that as a young child, Irvin often cried himself to sleep but never gave a reason for it, and they were unaware as to why. While he was a student in high school, he began lighting fires, but there seldom was any significant damage. Whenever he was asked why he lit the fires he just shrugged and gave no explanation.

A psychologist who assessed Irvin after his arrest found that he had a low sex drive, and had a strong need to be validated. To Irvin, he was a guy who played on the football team. Everything seemed to be in contrast when it came to the personality and behavior of Irvin leading up to and including the murder spree.

One of the strangest stories that came about throughout the interviews was from a meter reader who had gone to the home of Irvin's mother. Normally, the back door was unlocked but on this occasion, at the height of the murder spree, it was locked.

When Irvin's mother answered the door, she stated, "With all this killing around here I'm locking that door from now on."

Sitting at her kitchen table, smiling was Irvin.

Irvin's Timeline

April 2, 1924

Leslie Irvin was born.

December 2, 1954

Shot and killed Mary Holland during a robbery.

December 23, 1954

Shot and killed Wesley Kerr during a robbery.

March 21, 1955

Shot and killed Wilhelmina Sailer during a robbery at her home.

March 28, 1955

Goebel Duncan, shot and killed along with Raymond Duncan and Elizabeth Duncan. His wife Mamie survived her injuries.

April 8, 1955

Irvin is arrested and charged with murder.

January 20, 1956

Irvin escaped from the Gibson County Jail in Princeton, Indiana.

February 9, 1956

Irvin is arrested again.

June 5, 1961

The court reverses his conviction.

June 13, 1962

Second trial is completed, Irvin found guilty.

November 9, 1983

Irvin dies of lung cancer.

CHAPTER 3:
Wayne Williams - The Atlanta Child Murders

As far as serial killers go, Williams is one that goes against the normal conditions of being classified as a serial killer. To be categorized as such, a person has to have carried out at least three murders. Williams was only ever convicted of committing two, but he was and still is, the main suspect in so many more.

The Atlanta Child Murders were a devastating set of events that took place in a poor, predominantly black, neighborhood in Atlanta. One by one, children were disappearing and turning up dead the following day. The community was in absolute terror, afraid to let their children out, and arming themselves with bats at night in case the killer came for their child. There were rumors of a white man carrying out the killings, and even the KKK being involved.

But, when Williams became the prime suspect, people were completely shocked. Here was a black man, well known in the community, allegedly killing all these little black children. How could it be true? Why would he hurt his own people in such a horrendous way? Thirty years later he's still claiming he's innocent. But what can't be ignored, is that following his incarceration, there were no more children murdered in the neighborhood. Coincidence?

Early Years

Wayne Bertram Williams, only child of Homer and Faye, was born in the Dixie Hills area of southwest Georgia on May 27, 1958. Homer and Faye were both teachers, and although little is known about Williams' childhood, it is believed to have been considered normal. Williams was a good student and by the time he graduated from high school, he had developed a strong interest in both journalism and radio.

His parents fully supported their son in any endeavor he chose to embark on, and financed his dreams of being a big star in the entertainment industry. His first radio station was created in his parent's home when he was just sixteen years old.

Williams followed his interest in radio and eventually created his own carrier current radio station. He spent a lot of his time at various radio stations, including WIGO and WAOK. It was through these stations that he developed friendships with several of the announcers and he began to venture into the fields of pop music production and management.

Convinced that he would find the next major recording star, Williams focused on the young black boys in the neighborhood, creating demo recordings at the expense of his parents. Unfortunately Williams did not have a good enough ear to be able to pick out boys with actual real talent. Despite not having any success, Williams spread tales around town that he had major recording deals in the pipeline and that he knew just the right people to make it big in the industry.

Williams continued to live at home with his parents, and he had only a few friends. He developed a habit of impersonating law enforcement, and in 1976 he was arrested for it. His car even had red lights under the grille and flashing blue lights on the dashboard. Although he was arrested and charged for impersonating a police officer, he was never convicted.

Although Williams could be construed as being a bit odd, and a well-established liar, there was nothing in his background or behavior to suggest he would become a violent criminal. But, that's exactly what happened.

Splash from a Bridge

In 1979, numerous children had disappeared, their bodies eventually surfacing after they had been horribly murdered. By 1981, a staggering 29 children had been killed, which lead to full-scale surveillance of the neighborhood by law enforcement. The community was heartbroken and terrified of who could possibly be committing such awful killings of their beloved children. At the time, Williams was not even in the line of sight as a potential suspect, given he had no history of violence, but all that changed in May 1981.

A surveillance team had been stationed near a bridge that spanned the Chattahoochee River, a common body disposal site of the murdered children, when the officers heard a very loud splash in the water below. They immediately stopped the first vehicle that crossed the bridge, and behind the wheel was Williams. He was questioned as to what he was doing on the bridge at night and he claimed he was on his way to audition a singer Cheryl Johnson, and he provided a phone number. It was later discovered that not only was the phone number fake, so was Cheryl Johnson - she didn't exist.

The body of Nathanial Cater, 27, was discovered two days later on May 24, in the river. He had been missing for three days, and his autopsy showed he had most likely died of asphyxia. The medical examiner was unable to say categorically that Nathanial had actually been strangled; only that he has suffocated in some manner.

The discovery brought Williams back into focus again, as police came to the conclusion that the loud splash they heard on the bridge that night was Williams disposing of Nathaniel's body. He was brought in for questioning again, and was subsequently put through three polygraph tests, of which he failed them all. Fiber and hair evidence found on two unsolved murder victims were matched to those found in Williams' car, home and his pet dog.

Detectives spoke to several of Williams' co-workers and were told that at the time of both murders Williams was suspected of committing, he was seen with numerous scratches on his arms and on his face. It was then believed that these could have been the result of the victims fighting back as they were being killed.

The investigation continued for several weeks, during which time Williams would hurl insults and make jokes at the officers staking out his residence. Williams at one point held a press conference outside his home to declare his innocence, but he also told reporters that he had failed the lie detectors, an odd admission to say the least.

Finally, on June 21, 1981, Williams was arrested for the murders of Nathaniel Cater and Jimmy Ray Payne, 29, a second victim that had been matched to Williams through the forensic evidence.

Arrest and Trial for Two Kills

On January 6, 1982, Williams went on trial for the two murders. The trial lasted for two months, during which the prosecutors showed they had matched nineteen different sources of fiber from the victims to his home. Matches were made with his bathroom, bedspread, clothes, gloves, carpets and his dog, not only to the two victims he was on trial for, but also several of the murdered children.

Further evidence provided to the court included eyewitness

testimony that put Williams in contact with many of the murder victims before they were killed. Williams had also given false and inaccurate details about his whereabouts at the time of the murders. Williams decided to take the stand during his trial which backfired after he became angry and argumentative, which did not show him in a good light to the jury.

The jury took just twelve hours to come to an agreement and verdict. On February 27, they announced Williams to be guilty of the murders of Nathaniel Cater and Jimmy Ray Payne. As a result, he was sentenced to life imprisonment. Later, in the 1990s, Williams requested a retrial but his appeal was denied. He made the appeal again in 2004, but again, a federal judge rejected his request for a retrial.

Atlanta Child Murders

Beginning in the summer of 1979, children were disappearing in Dixie Hills and turning up dead days later. The first two known victims were Edward Hope Smith and Alfred Evans. They had gone missing four days apart from each other, and were both found on July 28. Edward had been shot to death with a .22-caliber weapon. Alfred was killed most likely due to asphyxiation, according to the medical examiner. This was the start of a series of killings that would become known as the Atlanta Child Murders.

The next child to be killed was Milton Harvey. He disappeared while on his way to the bank to pay a bill for his mother, on September 4, 1979. His body was discovered three weeks later, and the medical examiner was unable to determine the cause of death. A little over a month later, October 21, Yusuf Bell was going to the store to run an errand for his neighbor. After his disappearance a witness claimed she had seen the youth get into a blue car on the day he went missing. His body was found in the grounds of an abandoned elementary school on November 8, 1979. He had been strangled to death.

On March 4, 1980, Angel Lenair went missing, and when her body was found six days later, she was confirmed as the first female victim of the Atlanta Child Murderer. When her body was discovered, she was tied to a tree, and had been strangled with an electrical cord and most likely sexually assaulted. A pair of panties that did not belong to her was found in her throat. The next victim, Jeffery Mathis, disappeared on March 11 while doing an errand for his mother. His body wasn't found until 11 months after his death.

On May 18, Eric Middlebrooks received a phone call from someone who has not been identified, and he left the house. The next day, his body was found, and his death was due to head injuries that had been inflicted with a blunt object.

Christopher Richardson was going to a local pool on June 9 when he disappeared. Then, on June 22, Latonya Wilson was kidnapped from her home, which brought in Federal agents due to the nature of the abduction. The following day, Aaron Wyche also disappeared. His body was discovered underneath a railroad trestle on June 24. Initially his death was considered an accident, but there were too many similar features to the other killings so he was added to the now long list of murdered children. By now the community was panic stricken, not only because of the children that were disappearing and turning up dead, but also because of the speed at which they were going missing.

On July 6, 1980, Anthony Carter was playing near his house when he disappeared. His body was found the next day, and he had suffered multiple stab wounds, resulting in his death. Earl Terell was killed while on his way to the local pool on July 30. His remains weren't discovered until January 9, 1981, and by then were comprised of only skeletal remains so the cause of death could not be determined.

Clifford Jones was abducted on August 20 and murdered. His body was found in October, and during the investigation five witnesses were uncovered who all pointed the finger at a specific perpetrator. They all claimed it was a particular white man who was later jailed in 1981 for aggravated sodomy and attempted rape. The witnesses gave details of the murder of Clifford including the condition of his body, but the detectives chose to add him to the list along with the other murdered children.

On September 14, Darron Glass disappeared from nearby his home. His body has never been found, so although it is not known for sure he was killed by the same man, the coincidences allow his disappearance to be considered related to the Atlanta Child Murders. The next victim was Charles Stephens, who went missing on October 9. The next day, his body was found and his death was deemed to be due to asphyxiation. On October 18, the remains of previous victim Latonya Wilson were found, but due to the state of the body her cause of death could not be determined.

Aaron Jackson went missing on November 1, and his body was found the following day. He too had died from asphyxiation. Then, on November 10, Patrick Rogers disappeared. His remains lay undiscovered until February 1981, and the medical examiner identified his skull had been crushed by multiple blows by something heavy.

No killings took place throughout December, but the reign of terror was not over. On January 3, 1981, Lubie Geter disappeared and was found strangled to death two days later. Lubie's friend, Terry Pue, disappeared on January 22. His body was found the following day, and he had been strangled with an object such as rope or cord. At the time of his autopsy, police stated they had been able to lift fingerprints from Terry's body but they were never put on file.

Patrick Baltazar went missing on February 6, and a week later, his body was found which showed signs of strangulation by ligature. The remains of Jeffrey Mathis were found close by. On

February 19, Curtis Walker was strangled to death and his body was discovered the very same day. Then, on March 2, Joseph Bell was killed by asphyxiation. Timothy Hill disappeared on March 11, and was initially recorded as a victim of drowning.

The first adult victim added to the list of murdered children was Larry Rogers, 20, who was killed on March 30. His murder was linked to the others because he had been asphyxiated, like many of those victims had been. The second adult added to the list was Eddie Duncan, whose body was found on March 31, but the medical examiner was unable to determine the cause of his death. Another adult, Michael McIntosh was found asphyxiated on April 1 and added to the list.

There were a number of other murder victims that were ruled out as being related even though there were many similarities between the cases. For example, Faye Yearby, 22, was killed in January 1981, and her body was found in similar circumstances to the discovery of Angel Lenair. Like Angel, Faye had been tied to a tree by the killer with her hands behind her back. She had also been stabbed to death like other victims on the official list. Yet, police at the time didn't consider her to be a victim of the same killer because she was too 'old' and she was female.

In April 1981, a spokesperson for the FBI made the astonishing claim that several of the murders were 'substantially solved' and suggestions were made that some of the children had been killed by their own parents. Naturally this caused extreme outrage throughout the community, that such a suggestion had even been made. At the same time, the leader of the Congress of Racial Equality, Roy Innis, brought forward to the public a story that had been told by a witness to the murders. This female witness claimed the children were murdered by a cult that was involved in Satanism, pornography and drugs.

Innis led a group of searchers to an area described by the witness that was allegedly the ritual site. There they found large inverted crosses, which seemingly backed up the story told by the witness. She was given two polygraph examinations, both of which she passed, but police had by then become focused on one specific suspect. This narrowed scrutiny led to the exclusion of all other possible suspects.

Jimmy Ray Payne was reported missing on April 22. The body of Jimmy was found six days later, and his death was due to asphyxiation, which prompted police to add him to the list. On May 11, William Barrett disappeared, and his body was discovered the next day, another apparent victim of asphyxiation.

Quite a number of the bodies had been discovered in the local rivers, which is what led police to stake out the Chattahoochee River the night Williams became the number one suspect.

List of Child Victims

- July 21, 1979 - Edward Smith, age 14
- July 25, 1979 - Alfred Evans, age 13
- September 4, 1979 - Milton Harvey, age 14
- October 21, 1979 - Yusef Bell, age 9
- March 4, 1980 - Angel Lenair, age 12
- March 11, 1980 - Jeffery Mathis, age 10
- May 18, 1980 - Eric Middlebrooks, age 14
- June 9, 1980 - Christopher Richardson, age 12
- June 22, 1980 - Latonya Wilson, age 7
- June 23, 1980 - Aaron Wyche, age 10
- July 6, 1980 - Anthony Carter, age 9
- July 30, 1980 - Earl Terell, age 11
- August 20, 1980 - Clifford Jones, age 13
- September 14, 1980 - Darren Glass, age 10
- October 9, 1980 - Charles Stephens, age 12
- November 1, 1980 - Aaron Jackson, age 9
- November 10, 1980 - Patrick Rogers, age 16
- January 3, 1981 - Lubie Geter, age 14
- January 22, 1981 - Terry Pue, age 15
- February 6, 1981 - Patrick Baltazar, age 11
- February 19, 1981 - Curtis Walker, age 15
- March 2, 1981 - Joseph Bell, age 15
- March 13, 1981 - Timothy Hill, age 13

Williams is Number 1 Suspect

Although Williams was only ever charged with the murders of Cater and Payne, he is considered to be the number one suspect in the Atlanta Child Murders. By some accounts, he was a violent homosexual who also was disgusted with his own black race. The prosecuting attorney at his trial went so far as to claim Williams was determined to wipe out future generations of black people by killing the children before they could breed and produce children.

One witness testified that he had seen Williams and Nathaniel Cater holding hands on the night Cater was killed. Another witness stated Williams had paid him two dollars for allowing Williams to fondle his genitals. However, despite the testimony from several witnesses that Williams was homosexual, there were other witnesses that testified Williams had normal sexual relations with women as well.

During his trial, the presiding judge allowed the prosecution to provide testimony on ten deaths from the list of child murders, in order to show a pattern between the Atlanta Child Murders and the murders of Nathaniel Cater and Jimmy Ray Payne.

The pattern cases involved the murders of:

- Alfred Evans
- Eric Middlebrooks
- Charles Stephens

- William Barrett
- Terry Pue
- John Porter
- Lubie Geter
- Joseph Bell
- Patrick Baltazar
- Larry Rogers

These cases were considered a pattern because they consisted of the following similarities:

- Victim was a black male
- Clothing from the victim was missing
- No car
- Families of the victims were poor
- No evidence victim had been abducted forcefully
- Broken or dysfunctional home
- No explanation or identified motive for disappearance of victim
- Williams claimed he had no contact with victim
- Death by asphyxia due to strangulation
- No valuables found
- Body found near expressway ramp or major artery roadway
- Street hustlers
- Disposal of body unusual
- Transported either before death or after
- Similar fibers found on body

The most important evidence produced during Williams' trial was of course the large amount of fiber and hair that linked Williams to the bodies of several murder victims. Some of the fibers found on several bodies were the same as carpet fibers found inside the Williams home. However, the prosecution failed to inform the courtroom that the majority of the fibers found to be a match were actually very common, and could be found in carpets in homes and businesses throughout Atlanta.

"I'm Innocent"

Right from the beginning Williams has vowed and declared he is innocent. Although this isn't uncommon amongst prison inmates, after all, most will claim they are innocent, in the case of Williams, there is enough controversy surrounding the case that the question of his true innocence has been fought on both sides throughout his incarceration.

Williams and his lawyers claimed the murder conviction was a miscarriage of justice that has resulted in him spending most of his adult life in prison while the real murderer has gone free. They made the suggestion that the Atlanta officials even covered up evidence of Ku Klux Klan involvement in the murders so they could pin the crimes on Williams. It must be said however, that from the time of Williams' arrest and conviction, there were no further children being murdered.

As the appeals process progressed, Justice Richard Bell was

assigned by the Georgia Supreme Court to draft the opinion of Williams' case and conviction. Bell concluded that Williams did not receive a fair trial, and that the decision to convict Williams should have been reversed. But when Bell's opinion was reviewed by the full court, the vote was not in favor. The draft written by Bell was then rewritten, and Bell was allegedly pressured to change his vote to uphold the conviction.

Bell's original draft criticized the presiding judge for allowing the prosecution team to link Williams to the deaths of John Porter, Eric Middlebrooks, Charles Stephens, Alfred Evans and Patrick Baltazar, as the standards for identifying the links were not met. Bell stated that "there was no evidence placing Williams with those five victims before their murders, and as in all the murders linked to Williams, there were no eyewitnesses, no confession, no murder weapons and no established motive. Also, the five deaths, while somewhat similar to each other in technique, were unlike the two for which Williams was tried."

By linking the other murders to those of Cater and Payne, the presumption of Williams being innocent was effectively removed. According to Bell's report, "because the evidence of guilt as to the two charged offenses was wholly circumstantial, and because of the prejudicial impact of the five erroneously admitted (uncharged) homicides must have been substantial, we cannot say that it is highly probable that the error did not contribute to the jury's verdict."

Justice George Smith refused to change his vote, even though Bell felt he was pressured to change his. Justice Smith stated that by allowing the other murder cases to be presented during the trial, it "illustrates the basic unfairness of this trial and Williams' unenviable position as a defendant who, charged with two murders, was forced to defend himself as to 12 separate killings."

As the years have passed since the murders and Williams' incarceration, more people who were connected with the case have swayed towards believing Williams is innocent. Even some of the victim's relatives have changed their opinions over time to side with Williams. Atlanta detective and now DeKalb County Sheriff Sidney Dorsey was one of the first to search the home of Williams after the murders, and he has said that, "Most people who are aware of the child murders believe as I do that Wayne Williams did not commit these crimes."

A number of organizations were suggested as being responsible for the child murders, including the Ku Klux Klan, the FBI and the CIA. There was genuine fear in the community that the Klan was trying to instigate a race war by killing the black children. An informant claimed the Klan had tried to recruit him, and that member Charles Sanders had told him that this was their plan. However, the argument against the Klan being involved came down largely to the method of the murders.

The Klan were certainly not above killing children to make their point, after all they quite happily blew up churches. But, there is a big difference between blowing up an establishment or vehicle with explosives to actually strangling individual children. In a community that consisted of a black majority, a white person roaming the area would have been obvious as being out of place, especially with everyone in a heightened state of alert as they were as their children started to disappear.

Recent Developments

Although Williams was the main suspect in at least 24 murders, he was only ever charged and convicted of two. This was over 30 years ago, and at that time, DNA testing was yet to be invented and perfected. At best, when these crimes were committed, scientists could only identify blood type and match fibers, a large proportion of what sent Williams to jail for those two murders.

In 2010, DNA testing was used for the first time to try and link Williams to one of the victims conclusively. The victim was Patrick Baltazar, an 11 year old boy who was found murdered and dumped behind an office area on February 13, 1981. When his body was found, two human hairs were found inside his shirt.

When the trial took place, both police and the FBI testified that these scalp hairs matched Williams when looked at under a microscope. But because there was no DNA testing, this was purely a matter of opinion and judgement rather than actual scientific proof. Along with the human hairs, there were also a number of dog hairs found on the other victims, and in 2007, the defense lawyers for Williams questioned the validity of DNA testing the dog hairs to see if they really did come from Williams' dog.

The human scalp hairs were sent to the FBI's DNA laboratory at Quantico, Virginia, for testing. The tests showed that the hairs had the same type of DNA sequence as the hair from Williams' head, and approximately 98% of the population was eliminated. The laboratory was unable to say that the hair was definitely from Williams, but given the vast number of people who could be eliminated, that last 2% definitely contained Williams as a possible donor of the hairs.

To be more exact, the FBI held 1, 148 hair samples from African-American persons in their database, and when they were compared to the hairs from the body of Baltazar, only 29 of those samples had the same DNA sequence. Therefore the contributor of the evidential hairs fit into only 2 ½ of every 100 African-Americans.

The samples from Hispanics and Caucasians were ruled out, but when they are added into the total, the odds against Williams rise to nearly 130 to 1. It's important to note that the hairs they were testing from Baltazar's body were incomplete, and did not contain enough material to test for nucleic DNA. This nucleic

DNA testing includes the lineage of the father, and is a more effective way of determining who the DNA contributor is. The hairs were tested for mitochondrial DNA which only traces the maternal lineage.

The dog hairs found on the body were sent to the School of Veterinary Medicine genetics laboratory at the University of California in 2007 for DNA testing. The results showed that Williams' dog Sheba had the same DNA sequence as the hairs provided as evidence. It further stated that the DNA chain would only be identified in 1 out of 100 dogs.

It is easy to glance at these results and be convinced that Williams was at least guilty of murdering Patrick Baltazar. But, in the context of the whole picture, these fiber and hair results are merely circumstantial. After all, it cannot be said categorically that the hairs came from the head of Williams, only that he couldn't be excluded. And as for the dog hairs, these too cannot be attributed solely to Williams' dog Sheba, only that it's a high probability. When it comes to proving guilt, a lot more is needed to secure a prosecution and conviction.

It's important to remember that Williams, although the number one suspect, was only ever charged and convicted of two murders, both of who were adults and not children. There has never been any motive for any of the crimes, and nothing in Williams' personality or background to indicate he was a serial killer. There is no proof he ever had contact with the victims before their deaths, and he has never claimed to be responsible for any murders. All the authorities have ever found is circumstantial evidence, and very little of it at that.

So, the question remains - was Williams the Atlanta Child Murderer? He was certainly the only suspect ever fully investigated, and still he couldn't be charged. There were no eyewitnesses to any of the crimes, and nobody has ever come forward with further information. One thing that is for certain is that once Williams was securely locked behind bars, there were no further murders of black children in the area. Is that simply a coincidence or was Williams really the Atlanta Child Murderer.

Interview with Williams in 1991

"I cry. I break down. But you will never see me banging my head against the wall. Not me."

These are the words spoken by Williams during an interview in 1991, while he was incarcerated. By that stage he had been imprisoned for ten years. When he was asked about his life in prison all those years, he stated, ""I guess one reason that I can do this 'time' in such a content manner is because by the age I was when I was arrested . . . I had pretty much lived, I guess you could say, a fuller life than a lot of people do with regular 9-to-5s by the time they reach 40. I had done a lot of things in my life, worked a lot of different careers that I enjoyed. I enjoyed that time because it was quality years, so I really didn't miss out on a lot."

He later amended his statement in the interview stating, "'Content' is the wrong word altogether. Let's just face it - nobody can be content with this mess."

While in prison, Williams had come into contact with brothers of some of the child victims who happened to be fellow inmates. With the brothers of victims Patrick Rogers and Jefferey Mathis, Williams shared the case files he had with them, and they reached a 'good understanding' between them.

As well as the relatives he had met while incarcerated, Williams also made contact with the mothers of some of the child victims. Without going into detail about what was discussed with them, he did say, "I truly hope they find out who killed their children."

After spending ten years in prison, Williams said the only thing that changed is age, and that it had tempered him and made him a little wiser. "Very few things worry me to the point of getting me upset, and that helps to defuse a lot of tense situations. 'Carefree' would be the wrong word. I'm a very light-hearted person. It's almost like the class clown. You could put me in that category. That's me."

Williams stated that if he was ever set free, the first thing he would try to improve was the conditions in the Georgia correction system. Then he may pursue the ministry. "I know eventually, that I'm gonna get out."

"All I want is for society to see me for the individual I am and not the creation that was necessary for the state to get a conviction."

"If you look at the case group, you'll see no serial killer," Wayne Williams says. "You didn't have one general pattern, [but] two or three sub-groups with several suspects. Some were money-for-sex: Joseph Bell, Hill, Baltazar and Angel Lenair. Some were street crime like Middlebrooks, Porter, Evans and Smith. And, we'll probably find out, Payne and Cater. Then some were plain psycho murders like Yusef Bell and Clifford Jones."

The Psychological Assessment that Wasn't

As part of the preparations for the trial, the defense team brought in a psychologist, Dr. Brad Bayless, to assess Williams' mental state over a period of three interviews. But, when Williams heard the results he refused to let the doctor testify. Why? Because Dr. Bayless had come to some conclusions regarding his sexuality, and he was unwilling to adjust his formal report.

Dr. Bayless stated that he thought Williams was capable of committing a murder, but that he couldn't have acted alone in the multiple murders of the children in Atlanta. He said, "'I strongly believe -- it's my opinion -- that Wayne is not capable of doing this all by himself. There will be others implicated in this down the road."

Regarding the sexual content of his report, Dr. Bayless said, "He got very upset with me about whole sexual arena. "I was going to testify that Wayne was primarily asexual, had not had any success in either heterosexual or homosexual activity."

The fact that Williams refused to let him testify was a big mistake in the doctor's opinion. This was because the prosecution had presented to the jury that Williams was a closet homosexual. Witnesses were brought in to say that Williams had made homosexual passes at them, but according to Dr. Bayless, Williams didn't have the capability to seduce either a male or a female.

His assessment of Williams also concluded that Williams had a 'tremendous need for power, to have control'. He also could not tolerate anything that showed him in a negative light. Williams was known to lie about things just to make himself look better.

"Wayne, like anyone else under certain conditions, has the capability of killing. However, the better question is; can a person, without being threatened have enough internal anger to commit a crime or commit a murder type situation?" He then added that Williams had a 'lot of frustration, a lot of anger and a lot of resentment, which began to manifest itself within him as he grew out of childhood'.

Although there had been reports that Williams had an IQ of 136, Dr. Bayless said he wasn't a genius at all. Also, he wasn't showing any signs of being psychotic or mentally unstable.

'"Wayne had a lot of problems, I think, with putting faith in other people because of his own egocentric thoughts. He doesn't see anyone more capable than himself. Wayne has contempt for individuals who he sees ... being less than himself.

He tends to be rather condescending at times."

"Wayne was a late child, born to parents in their mid-40s," he said. "As he grew and developed, it appeared from his history that in early development years, he was rather picked on and really kind of used as scapegoat by other children. For example, he would have to wait after school for parents - who were school teachers -- were ready to leave instead of going home with other kids -- which set him up for lot of criticism, teasing from other children."

Did He Act Alone?

Even the defense psychologist felt that Williams was incapable of carrying out the dozens of murders on his own, and he certainly wasn't alone in that thought. Many in the community wondered if there was more than one killer, that perhaps Williams had accomplices to help him, which would explain how he was able to carry out these terrible crimes without being detected. There are even rumors that perhaps the two adult men Williams was convicted of killing were in fact his accomplices, and maybe they had decided to turn on him so he got rid of them.

Another rumor that was rampant was that Williams was a 'procurer' of young children for a pornography ring in the area. Perhaps he was paid to lure the youngsters away and left them with perverts to do with them as they chose. This would mean

Williams wasn't the actual murderer, he just supplied the victims.

Timeline Including Alleged Crimes

1958

Born in Dixie Hills neighborhood of Atlanta.

1973

Williams worked for WIGO radio as an announcer.

1974

Started his own radio station from home.

1976

Graduated from High School with honors. Arrested for impersonating a police officer but wasn't convicted. Worked for WBJE radio as a reporter and announcer.

1977

Enrolled at Georgia State University. Worked for WGST radio as a researcher.

1978

Charged with making a false charge, but case was dismissed.

1979

Dropped out of University. Worked as a photographer with WSB-TV. Alfred Evans found strangled to death. Edward Hope Smith also found murdered. Yusef Bell found strangled to death.

1980

Eric Middlebrooks found beaten to death. Christopher Richardson is murdered. Aaron Wyche found with a broken neck. Anthony Carter found stabbed to death. Earl Terrell found deceased. Clifford Jones found strangled and beaten to death. Charles Stephens suffocated to death. Aaron Jackson killed by suffocation. Patrick Rogers found deceased from trauma to the head.

1981

Terry Pue found strangled to death. Lubie Geter found deceased from strangulation. Patrick Baltazar found dead. Timothy Hill suffocated to death. Eddie Duncan found deceased. Larry Rogers suffocated to death. John Porter stabbed to death. Joseph Bell found deceased. Michael McIntosh found murdered. Jimmy Payne killed by asphyxiation. William Barrett found deceased. Interrogated by the police. Nathaniel Carter found deceased. Williams arrested and charged.

1982

Trial begins. Found guilty on 2 counts of murder. First appeal denied.

1983

Second appeal denied.

1985

Third appeal denied.

1999

Fourth appeal denied.

2000

Fifth appeal denied.

2001

Sixth appeal denied.

2006

Seventh appeal denied.

Eighth appeal denied.

2007

Ninth appeal denied.

CHAPTER 4:
The Connecticut River Valley Killer

This is perhaps one of the most baffling and terrifying cases of serial murder in Claremont, and maybe even in the whole of the United States. A series of shocking murders were taking place, and nobody knew who was doing it. The victims were all women, and all were killed in frenzied, violent attacks.

Even though there were survivors of these attacks, the identity of the killer remains unknown. Though there have been several suspects over the years, and one in particular is considered more likely than the others. But with the death of the main suspect went any chance of getting a confession, which has left a mystery that is still very much on the minds of investigators today.

Who was the Connecticut River Valley killer, and what happened to him? Is he still alive today? Did he move away and carry out murders elsewhere without detection? Could modern-day forensic science finally solve the puzzle?

Missing Women

During the 1980's, the disappearance of three women around the Claremont area would eventually lead to the discovery of a serial killer who had likely been operating for quite some time beforehand. The remains of two female victims were found in 1981 and 1985, within 1000 feet of each other, in the woods in Kellyville, New Hampshire.

The decomposition of one set of remains made it difficult for the medical examiner to determine the cause of death, but there were some indicators that suggested the woman had been stabbed multiple times. The autopsy of the second set of remains showed evidence of multiple stab wounds. In between the discovery of these two victims, a third woman had been stabbed to death in her home in Saxtons River, Vermont, in what was described as a frenzied attack. Just ten days later, the remains of the fourth woman who had gone missing were discovered. Again, the autopsy showed she had most likely been stabbed multiple times.

Now with four potentially linked cases, investigators began to question whether there had been any previous murders that were similar. They uncovered two cases that matched, one in 1978 and the other in 1981. This further encouraged investigators to believe there was a serial killer in the area. As more murders took place, and with other non-fatal attacks that were almost identical in nature, investigators were able to find similarities in the modus operandi, dump sites and patterns in the manner of stab wounds, that suggested they were right in thinking a serial killer was responsible.

Known Murders and Survivors

Cathy Millican

The first known victim of the Connecticut River Valley Killer was Cathy Millican. Cathy, aged 27, went missing on October 24, 1978, while photographing birds in New London, New Hampshire. The following day, her body was found just yards away from where she had last been seen. The medical examiner discovered she had suffered 29 stab wounds, leading to her death.

Mary Elizabeth Critchley

The next known victim, Mary Elizabeth Critchley, disappeared on July 25, 1981, near Interstate 91 at the Massachusetts-Vermont border. The 37 year old had been hitchhiking to Waterbury in Vermont when she went missing. Her body was eventually found on August 9, in a wooded area in Unity, New Hampshire. Unfortunately the medical examiner was unable to determine her cause of death due to the condition of her body when it was found.

Bernice Courtemanche

Bernice Courtemanche, just 16 years old, was last seen on May 30, 1984, in Claremont. Her boyfriend's mother was the last person to see Bernice, a nurse's aide, and believed she was going to hitchhike along Route 12 in New Hampshire to go and see her boyfriend. Her body was later found in April 1986, by a fisherman. The autopsy performed on her remains showed evidence of wounds to the neck caused by a knife and an injury to her head.

Ellen Fried

Ellen Fried, 27, was a supervising nurse at Valley Regional Hospital, and she disappeared on July 20, 1984. She had driven to a payphone in Claremont to call her sister. While on the phone, she told her sister a strange car had been driving back and forth. She left the phone to see if her car would start, then went back to the phone and spoke to her sister for a few more minutes. Ellen failed to turn up to work the next day, and her car was discovered abandoned a few miles away from the payphone she had used the night before. Her body was eventually found in September, and showed evidence of multiple stabbing wounds and she was probably sexually assaulted.

Eva Morse

The next suspected victim was Eva Morse, a 27 year old single mother, who disappeared on July 10, 1985. She had been hitchhiking near the border of Claremont and Charlestown, on Route 12, in New Hampshire. Her remains were found the following year, only 150 metres from where the remains of Mary Elizabeth Critchley were found in 1981. Eva's body was found to have knife wounds inflicted to the neck.

Lynda Moore

Lynda Moore, 36, was outside doing work in her yard in Saxtons River, Vermont, on April 15, 1986. Unlike the other victims so far, Lynda wasn't abducted and murdered elsewhere; her husband came home and found her stabbed to death. The investigation at the crime scene indicated there had been quite a fierce struggle between Lynda and her attacker. This time there were witness reports of a man being seen loitering near her home on the day of her murder. The suspect was described as being dark haired, stocky built, around 20 - 25 years old, clean shaven and wearing dark-rimmed glasses. He was also seen wearing a blue knapsack. It wasn't until the following year that a composite sketch was publicly released.

Barbara Agnew

On January 10, 1987, Barbara Agnew, 38, was on her way home after a skiing outing with friends in Stratton, Vermont, when she disappeared. Her vehicle was found by a snowplow driver at a rest stop on the I-91 in Hartford, Vermont, but she was nowhere to be seen. On inspection of the vehicle, blood could be seen on the steering wheel. Her body was found two months later, on March 28, near an apple tree in Hartland, Vermont. The autopsy showed she had been stabbed to death. One thing that always bothered investigators was why she had pulled into that rest stop during a snow storm in the first place.

Jane Boroski

There were no further murders after Barbara Agnew, and it seemed the killer had stopped. However, on the evening of August 6, 1988, another victim was attacked. Jane Boroski, 22 and seven months pregnant at the time, was driving home from a county fair in Keene, New Hampshire, and stopped at a convenience store in West Swanzey. The store was closed, but she was able to get a soda from a vending machine outside. As she returned to her vehicle, she noticed a Jeep Wagoneer parked beside her. She got into her vehicle and when she looked at the rear view mirror, she saw the driver of the Jeep walking around behind her vehicle. The man came up to her open window and asked if the payphone was working. Before she could respond he grabbed her and pulled her out of the vehicle.

As they struggled, the man accused Jane of beating up his girlfriend. He asked her if she had Massachusetts plates on her car, and she responded she had New Hampshire plates. This didn't stop the attack, and the man stabbed Jane 27 times before he took off in his vehicle. Remarkably, Jane managed to get back into her car and drive to friend's home for assistance. As she got close to the house though, she noticed the vehicle driving ahead of her was the Jeep.

Jane arrived at her friend's home, who immediately came to help her. They noticed the man in Jeep perform a U-turn up the road and slowly drove by the friend's house before finally speeding off. Jane was taken to the hospital and her injuries included a severed jugular vein, a laceration to the kidney, both lungs were collapsed, and tendons in her knees and thumb had been severed.

Jane's baby survived the attack but was later diagnosed with mild cerebral palsy, although it is not known if this was because of the attack and the injuries suffered by Jane or not. A composite sketch of the attacker was created with the help of Jane, and she was also able to give the police the first three characters of the Jeep's license plate. Unfortunately the investigation led nowhere and the case was eventually deemed cold.

In an effort to solve the case, detectives brought in John Philpin, a criminal psychologist, to develop a forensic profile of the killer. He made multiple visits to the area where the bodies of Bernice and Ellen were found, in an attempt to get a better understanding of how the killer's mind worked at the time of the killings. Philpin believed the killer had sites already picked out before he snatched his victims.

Jane was put under hypnosis by Philpin to see if more information was stored in her subconscious. She described the attack she endured in great detail, and said that the man attacking her seemed to be very calm and collected. Jane also stated that whenever she stopped struggling, her attacker seemed to lose interest in her and would stop attacking. She was able to describe the Jeep Wagoneer and provide 3 digits of the license plate.

The Main Suspects

Delbert Tallman

Tallman was initially considered a suspect because of a murder case he had previously been implicated in, and the locations he had resided in. The murder was of Heidi Martin, 16, who was killed on May 20, 1984, while she was out for a jog in Hartland, Vermont. The following day her body was found dumped in a swampy area behind the Hartland Elementary School. The young girl had been raped and then stabbed to death. Tallman, 21 at the time, confessed to committing the murder, but during his trial, he recanted his confession and was acquitted of the murder.

When the body of Barbara Agnew was discovered, it was just a mile away from where the body of Heidi Martin had been found. Tallman was known to have lived in the areas of Claremont, New Hampshire, Windsor, Vermont, and Bellows Falls, Springfield. These areas were considered to be the epicenter of the murders committed by the Connecticut River Valley Killer.

In 1996 Tallman was convicted of committing two counts of lewd and lascivious conduct with a child, and failure to comply with sex offender registration requirements. He was released from prison in October, 2010. Many people believe Heidi Martin's murder was committed by the Connecticut River Valley Killer, but to date, Tallman has not been implicated in any of the cases.

Michael Nicholaou

Michelle Marie Ashley disappeared in December 1988 from Vermont, along with her two children. Her mother contacted Lynn-Marie Carty, a private investigator, in 2001, seeking help on finding her daughter and her two grandchildren. She informed Carty that Michelle and the children had last been seen in the company of Michael Nicholaou, Michelle's common-law husband. This ultimately led to the investigation into Nicholaou and whether or not he was possibly the Connecticut River Valley Killer.

During the Vietnam War, Nicholaou served as a helicopter pilot with the U.S. Army. During his service he earned two Purple Hearts, two Silver Stars, and two Bronze Stars, but in 1970, he was charged along with seven of his fellow servicemen with murder and attempted murder charges. The charges related to the deaths of civilians during a reconnaissance mission in the Mekong Delta. Eventually the charges were dropped, but Nicholaou was still discharged and sent home in disgrace.

Following his return home, and for the rest of his life, he received treatment for posttraumatic stress disorder from the Veterans Administration. Some of his fellow Army colleagues later recalled Nicholaou as having left camp on one occasion at least, to seek hand-to-hand combat with the enemy, and stated that he was going hunting for humans.

Settled in Virginia, Nicholaou opened up a sex shop called The

Pleasure Chest, which drew a lot of attention from law enforcement. Twice the shop was raided, and Nicholaou and his partner were charged with selling obscene materials. When they went on trial, both were convicted on one occasion and for the second trial, it was declared a mistrial. It was while he was in Virginia that Nicholaou met Michelle Ashley. Shortly afterwards, they moved to Holyoke, Massachusetts, and went on to have their two children, Joy and Nick.

To Michelle's family Nicholaou appeared to be quiet and a bit strange. At one point during their marriage, Michelle attempted to leave Nicholaou, and fled with the children. Nicholaou contacted her family while in pursuit of Michelle. She subsequently returned to Nicholaou, telling her family she was fearful of him, and stated that she was intending to leave him for good.

Michelle's mother paid a visit to Michelle and Nicholaou's home in December 1988, because she hadn't heard from Michelle for several weeks. On entering the home, she found it vacant with no signs of Michelle, the children or Nicholaou, except for a baby book and rotten food in the refrigerator.

After Michelle's mother contacted investigator Carty, it didn't take long to track Nicholaou down, who was living in Georgia. He claimed he had no idea where Michelle was, that Michelle was a 'slut' who had been taking drugs and ran off leaving the children behind. He said the children were fine, which was confirmed the next day after a phone call with young Nick.

Nicholaou had remarried, and by 2005, his second wife Aileen had tried to escape the relationship after Nicholaou had allegedly attacked her. He found Aileen at her sister's home in Tampa, Florida, on December 31, 2005, and what ensued was a terrifying experience for all involved.

Nicholaou had arrived at the residence dressed in a black suit, carrying a guitar case which unfortunately did not contain a guitar but an arsenal of guns. He led Aileen, and his stepdaughter Terrin Bowman, 20, into one of the bedrooms while Aileen's sister fled to call the police. Sadly they didn't arrive in time, and Nicholaou shot Aileen, Terrin and then himself. Both Aileen and Nicholaou died at the scene and Terrin died a little while later in hospital.

Carty began investigating Nicholaou to see if there were any links between him and the Connecticut River Valley Killer. The murders had taken place around the same time as Michelle had disappeared. Of note, one of Nicholaou's ex-wives had been a nurse, as were three of the Connecticut River Valley victims. Also of interest, Nicholaou had lived in Holyoke which was around 90 miles from Claremont, and it was discovered Michelle had family in the area. In fact, a note was found in the abandoned baby book that put Michelle at the same hospital that victim Agnew disappeared from around the same time.

Another point of interest was the vehicle Nicholaou had owned on August 6, 1988 - a Jeep Wagoneer, the same vehicle described by Boroski as being driven by her attacker. Carty showed Boroski a photograph of Nicholaou, and she stated there was a resemblance between her attacker and Nicholaou.

The evidence that discredits Nicholaou as a possible suspect is perhaps why he has never been formally linked to the Connecticut River Valley murders. At the time of the murders of Courtemanche, Fried and Morse, Nicholaou had been living in Virginia. To date there is no physical evidence or even definitive circumstantial evidence to suggest Nicholaou was the notorious killer.

Gary Westover

Paraplegic Gary Westover, 46, told his uncle Howard Minnon, a retired Grafton County Sheriff's deputy that he had a confession to make in October 1997. Westover claimed that in 1987 he had been picked up by three friends to embark on a night of partying. He claimed they put him and his wheelchair into their van and they drove out to Vermont. There, they abducted, murdered and dumped the body of Barbara Agnew. Minnon was given the names of the three associates, and he shared the information with law enforcement, his wife, and his daughter.

At the time, Minnon didn't believe the authorities treated the information provided seriously, and nothing further came about from it. In March 1998 Westover died, and Minnon later died in 2006. In August of that year, Westover's aunt wrote a letter to the sister of Barbara Agnew, Anne, and shared the information from Westover's confession with her. Anne sent the letter on to Carty, and when Nicholaou's name was mentioned to Westover's aunt, she thought the name sounded familiar.

Speculation is that Nicholaou may have met Westover through their association with the Veteran's Hospital, but this has never been proven.

Other Possible Crimes

There have been several other murders that for one reason or another have been considered potential further victims of the Connecticut River Valley Killer. Although they are not confirmed cases, they are certainly worth considering.

Joanne Dunham

On June 11, 1968, Joanne Dunham, 14 was sexually assaulted and strangled to death in Charlestown, New Hampshire. Her case has been considered a potential victim because of the location of her murder.

Sylvia Gray

Sylvia Gray was 76 years old when she was found in a wooded area within a few hundred yards of her home on October 5, 1982. She had been reported missing the day before from Plainfield, New Hampshire. Sylvia had been brutally bludgeoned then stabbed to death.

Steven Hill

The last time Steven Hill, 38, was seen, he was on his way to get his paycheck from his employer in Lebanon, New Hampshire. It was June 20, 1986, and his body was eventually found on July 15 in Hartland, across the river from where Sylvia Gray's body had previously been found. Steven had suffered multiple stab wounds, leading to his death.

Unknown Woman

A shocking discovery was made beside the Massachusetts Route 78 in Warwick, Massachusetts, on June 24, 1988. The decomposing arms and legs of an unknown woman had been found less than a mile away from the border of New Hampshire. The torso and the head have never been located, and it is believed they were disposed of at another site. Although the victim's identity has not been uncovered, she was described as being a white woman, of average height, and an athletic body type.

Carrie Moss

Another young victim, Carrie Moss, 14, disappeared on July 25, 1989, from New Boston, New Hampshire. She had left the home she shared with her parents and was making her way to see friends in Goffstown. Two years later, almost to the day, her remains were found, on July 24, 1991. She had been disposed of in a wooded area in New Boston. Due to the level of decomposition, the cause of death could not be determined, but it was believed she died as the result of a homicidal act.

The Case Goes Cold

Although a lot of information had been gathered about all of the murders and the potential suspects, the Connecticut River Valley Killer case went cold. A task force had been formed at the time of the murders, and with assistance from John Philpin, a criminal profiler, they were able to identify potential suspects but it couldn't be developed any further.

There has been quite a lot of media attention over the years which has brought the case back into the spotlight on numerous occasions, yet nobody has been able to identify the composite sketches of the alleged killer. Books have been written, and segments have been aired on television, still to no avail.

There are a number of reasons as to why this case has yet to be solved. At the time when the murders were being committed, there was very little advancement in forensic science techniques. There was yet to be the breakthroughs in DNA technology that exist today. Although samples were most likely taken at the time, even the storage of such samples was second-rate compared to now, so many samples from that era would have deteriorated over time.

Another factor that has impeded the investigation is the time that has elapsed. Many of the main players, witnesses, suspects and other people involved in the case have since died, so it is impossible to get further information from them. This doesn't mean of course that the case can never be solved; it just means it is more complicated.

It is interesting that all of the murders associated with the Connecticut River Valley Killer ended with the attack on Jane Boroski. Perhaps the killer thought he had made too many errors with this attack, such as letting his vehicle be seen by witnesses as he stalkingly drove back and forth in front of the house where Jane sought shelter. If the attack on Jane was indeed the work of the Connecticut River Valley Killer, he had failed in his attempt to kill her, which undoubtedly would have angered him no end. Was that what made him stop? Because he had finally failed?

The Murder of Jessica Briggs

The belief that the Connecticut River Valley Killer had stopped his attacks may have been false all along. Former criminal profiler Gregg O. McCrary and fellow profiler John Philpin later stated that the murder of Jessica Briggs bore uncanny similarities to the murders of the other victims of the Connecticut River Valley Killer.

Jessica Briggs, 16, was murdered in 1989, and the injuries she sustained were similar to those inflicted on other Connecticut River Valley murder victims. However, a man was arrested, tried and convicted of Jessica's murder and recently the case has made major headlines, as the alleged killer fights to have his name cleared.

Anthony Sanborn Jr. has spent more than 25 years behind bars for the murder of Jessica Briggs, a crime he claims he was not responsible for. In April 2017, Sanborn was released on bail, as recent evidence and theories have added to the legitimacy of his claims. One of the most important pieces of evidence relates to a key witness in his original trial in 1992, who has since recanted her testimony. During the trial, the witness claimed she had seen Sanborn near the Maine State Pier at the time of Jessica's murder. Now, she states that not only was she never there, but she was also partially blind at the time so would have been incapable of seeing or recognizing Sanborn.

Sanborn's efforts to have his conviction overturned have been further fueled by the statements by profilers Gregg O. McCrary and John Philpin. They had stated in reports filed with the Criminal Court in Portland that the circumstances surrounding Jessica's murder were so similar to those of the killings committed by the Connecticut River Valley Killer, that they could actually be the work of the same man.

During Sanborn's second trial, an agreement was reached between Sanborn and the prosecution, and in November, 2017, Sanborn was freed from prison. Although his conviction still stands, the agreement allowed for Sanborn to be released under the terms of time already served, given he had served a substantial amount of his original 70 year sentence.

Survivor Boroski Identifies Nicholaou

In 2006, evidence was provided to Jane Boroski from a private investigator that in her mind, finally put a name to the face of the man who so viciously attacked her. She believes her attacker, and potentially the Connecticut River Valley Killer, was indeed Michael Nicholaou. She isn't alone in her suspicions, with some of the family members of other victims wanting Nicholaou to be either ruled in as a suspect or ruled out, so they can finally have some peace. But it's just not that simple.

Head of the homicide unit in the New Hampshire Attorney General's office in 2006, Jeff Strelzin, explained the issues surrounding DNA and forensic evidence from old cases. "There are often difficulties in older cases as far as locating the evidence and the condition of it. And the last thing is, were the samples obtained actually useful? Twenty years ago the technology was different than it exists today, so 20 years ago, people didn't take swabs for DNA like they do now. And things aren't necessarily stored in such a way that they would be useful for the testing we can do today."

For Boroski, the years that have passed since her attack have not been easy. She has had many issues with depression and even suicidal thoughts, and was hospitalized for these issues more than once. She said the attack left her very angry at a lot of things.

Her daughter, who survived the attack on Boroski while in utero, has struggles with mild cerebral palsy, affecting her learning, motor skills and speech.

"I've tried to make life normal for my kids. But it's always been in the back of my mind. Who did this? When is he going to get caught? Is he going to get caught? Is he dead? Is he in jail?"

When the private investigator, Lynn-Marie Carty, first made contact with Boroski it came out of the blue. She was sent a package containing information about Nicholaou, and photographs of him. At the time when Boroski was attacked, Nicholaou and his wife Michelle were fighting, and she packed up the kids and left. Nicholaou was driving up the same highway where Boroski was attacked at the same time, looking for his wife and children.

Once Boroski saw the series of photographs sent to her by Carty, she became convinced that Nicholaou was her attacker. Although his face didn't match the identikit sketch she had done all those years ago, she said she was never really happy with how the sketch came out, that it didn't resemble her attacker as well as she had hoped.

But, Chris Moore, who is the son of victim Lynda Moore, isn't so convinced. He agrees that the photographs of Nicholaou don't match the identikit drawing, but the description is very similar to the man seen in the driveway of his home the day his mother was killed. It is also known that the year before Boroski was sent the photographs, she saw his picture and stated that he was not the man who attacked her.

Now, she is convinced that it was him, and that she isn't mistaken. She said, "You just know. I just know it was him."

Samples of Nicholaou's blood are stored at the Medical Examiner's Office in Tampa, Florida. The DNA profile has been entered into the national database CODIS, but to date no matches have been made.

CHAPTER 5:
Michel Fourniret - The Ogre of the Ardennes

There is no killer more despised than the ones who kill children. Even in prison there is a sort of 'code' that makes child killers the bottom of the pack, often targets of violence, because killing a child somehow crosses an invisible line of what is acceptable amongst criminals.

Fourniret was one such killer. With the help of his wife, he abducted and tortured young girls, and inflicted upon them a bizarre and macabre 'medical' examination by his wife to determine if they were still virgins or not. Because Fourniret only wanted virgins. He hunted for them, searching for victims to quench his perverse fantasies.

He knew that the children were less likely to trust him, he was a dirty old man, but his wife had a look and manner that put them at ease. That's why it was so easy for them to abduct their victims. They crossed back and forth between France and Belgium, leaving crumpled innocent bodies in their wake. The question has to be asked, were there more victims out there that nobody but Fourniret and his wife know about?

Behind the Façade

Michel Fourniret was an experienced and qualified draughtsman, who went on to own his own business making tools near Paris by the time he was in his early 30's. But this talented handyman was not the good man that he portrayed to the outside world, which became evident when he was first arrested at the age of 24 for the abduction and abuse of a 10 year old girl in Sedan, in the Ardennes.

From then onwards, Fourniret's depraved side of his personality and character was truly beginning to flourish. He was convicted twice more of other crimes, then in 1984, he was arrested and charged with several kidnappings and sexual attacks on young women and teenage girls in Paris. For these hideous crimes he was placed in preventive detention, but rather than inhibit his fantasies, this enabled him to make contact with a woman who would later fuel his intentions and actions despite the horror of it all.

While incarcerated, Fourniret began a pen pal relationship with Monique Olivier, a woman who had been married twice before and had no contact with her own two children. Fourniret had placed an advertisement in the local Catholic magazine asking for a pen pal, and Olivier responded. Before long, they were corresponding regularly and intensely, and Olivier had developed a nickname of sorts for Fourniret, 'Shere Khan', the name of the tiger in the Jungle Book by Kipling. Other times she referred to Fourniret as her 'beast'.

As their letters continued to go back and forth, eventually they began discussing Fourniret's fantasies of raping virgins, and he offered referred to them as 'membranes on legs'. Olivier went along with the fantasies, even indulging in sharing some of her own surrounding the rape of young women with Fourniret. Unfortunately none of this correspondence came to light with the authorities until it was far too late to act upon.

Fourniret went on trial for the sexual assaults on 11 young girls, and in June 1987, he was sentenced to seven years in prison, with two of those years suspended. He had already served three years while waiting to go on trial, and because he had been deemed a model prisoner, he was released within just four months. On October 26, Fourniret exited the prison as free man, and waiting for him on the other side of the gate was Olivier. Within weeks of his release, Fourniret and Olivier would start hunting for their desired prey.

Hunting for Virgins

Fourniret and Olivier developed their modus operandi very early on, almost immediately after his release from prison. They had moved in together and had plenty of time to formulate their plan of how to get suitable victims and what to do with them once they were in their clutches. To the outside world, they looked like a regular, respectable, married couple, and this is what they decided to use to gain the trust of their young victims.

This deadly couple would drive around looking for the right target, then they would pull over and ask for directions. They would convince the young girl to get into their car, to show them how to get to where they needed to go, then once they had her, she would be bound and gagged and sometimes drugged. It was then up to Olivier to physically examine the girl to see if she was a virgin.

If the victim met the desired criteria, they would then be given to Fourniret so he could do whatever he pleased with them. Many of the girls were assaulted, then killed by either strangulation or gunshot. Disturbingly, Fourniret would refer to his victims as his 'beautiful little subjects'. The victims ranged between the ages of 12 and 21, and some crimes were committed in Belgium as well as France. Between 1987 and 2001, Fourniret and Olivier murdered multiple young girls and women.

Multiple Murders Committed

Fourniret later confessed to killing several victims, but it is believed there may be many more.

Isabelle Laville, 17

Isabelle was walking home from school in Auxerre on December 17, 1987, when she was abducted by Fourniret and Olivier. She was raped and killed, and it was later revealed that her body had been disposed of at the bottom of a well in northeastern France.

Farida Hellegouarch

Fourniret killed Farida, the girlfriend of a member of a gang of bank robbers who had once been a cellmate of his. Fourniret admitted he killed her so he could get hold of the gang's funds, with which he purchased his property in France.

Marie-Ange Domece, 19

Marie-Ange, a young mentally disabled woman, was killed in 1988. Her body has never been found, and Fourniret was a suspect for many years until he finally confessed to her murder.

Fabienne Leroy, 20

The couple kidnapped Fabienne from a supermarket car park in Chalons en Champagne, east of Paris, on July 8, 1988. The following day, her body was found near a local military base, and the autopsy revealed she had been injected with air into her veins then killed with a shotgun blast to her chest.

Jeanne-Marie Desramault, 22

A young law student, Jeanne-Marie was kidnapped from a train station in Charleville-Mezieres, on March 18, 1989. Her remains were later found buried in the grounds of a chateau in Donchery that Fourniret had previously owned.

Elisabeth Brichet, 12

The youngest known victim, Elisabeth was abducted while walking home from a friend's house in Namur, Belgium, on

December 20, 1989. Her remains were also buried at the chateau owned by Fourniret.

Joanna Parrish, 20

On the evening of May 16, 1990, Englishwoman Joanna disappeared from the town of Auxerre. The following day, her body was found in a nearby river. She had been raped and strangled to death.

Natacha Danais, 13

On November 21, 1990, Natacha had been shopping with her mother when she was kidnapped near Nantes, France. She was assaulted then stabbed to death, and three days later her body was found on a nearby beach.

Celine Saison, 18

Celine had just finished sitting an exam in high school in Charleville-Mezieres, when she disappeared. It was May 16, 2000, and her body was discovered two months later in a section of woods near the border of Belgium. She had been strangled to death.

Mananya Thumphong, 13

Mananya disappeared from the town of Sedan, France, on May 5, 2001. Her remains weren't located until a year later, in Nollevaux forest in Belgium, near the border.

Confessions of a Wife

In June, 2003, Fourniret and Olivier abducted a 13 year old girl in Ciney, Belgium, but remarkably, they failed to keep her captive. The brave young girl managed to chew through the ropes binding her, and when Fourniret stopped at a petrol station, she leapt from the van. A woman driving by rescued the young girl and managed to take down the registration number of Fourniret's van.

With the registration number and good description of her attackers, Belgian police wasted no time in finding Fourniret. He was arrested on June 26, 2003, and the French police were contacted and asked for a copy of Fourniret's previous arrest records. Despite a lengthy history of convictions, the French authorities claimed they couldn't find his records. But, the Belgian police were highly suspicious that Fourniret may have been responsible for other crimes.

One thing that bothered the investigators in Belgium was the elaborate set-up Fourniret had in his van for locking the doors. They also found a number of hairs in the van, which were sent off for analysis. They started to look at dozens of sex crimes that had been unsolved in both Belgium and France.

In June 2004, Olivier who had until then remained off the radar as a firm suspect, decided to come clean to the police about her husband's horrendous crimes he had been committing for nearly 20 years. This confession was spurred by the circumstances of another famous case that was in the courts at the time - murderer Marc Dutroux. It wasn't that Dutroux was on trial however, it was that his wife had been convicted and sentenced to 30 years for the part she played in the crimes. Therefore, Olivier figured that if she didn't come forward first, she would end up in the same boat.

After years of loyally supporting and assisting her husband in multiple rapes and murders, Olivier began to confess. She gave the police details of ten murders Fourniret had allegedly committed, including the dates and names of the victims. According to Olivier, eight of the victims were just teenagers. When confronted with his wife's allegations, Fourniret initially denied any involvement. But, eventually he gave in and confessed to nine of the murders. Despite her efforts, Olivier did not escape prosecution, and was also charged with murder and complicity in the murders of six others.

During Olivier's confession to the police, she gave further details about the murder of young Isabelle Laville. She claimed she was the one who had selected Isabelle because she looked similar to herself when she was younger. The fantasy was that Fourniret could imagine that it was a young virginal Olivier he was having sex with.

Olivier stopped the car beside Lavelle and asked her for directions. She managed to persuade Isabelle to get into the car so she could help Olivier find where she wanted to go. As they drove down the road, Fourniret was standing on the side of the road holding a fuel can, posing as a motorist who had broken down. Olivier stopped and picked him up.

Fourniret, seated in the back, put a rope around Isabelle's neck and informed her she was now his prisoner. They then gave her an overdose of sleeping pills. Back at their home, Fourniret was unable to rape Isabelle, so he had sex with Olivier instead. He then strangled Laville and disposed of her body down a disused well.

The next case Olivier talked about was the murder of Fabienne Leroy. By that time Olivier was heavily pregnant, and approached Fabienne claiming she needed to see a doctor urgently. When Fabienne got into the car, Fourniret was behind the wheel. He drove to a field and at gunpoint pulled Fabienne out of the car. Olivier checked her to see if she was a virgin, before Fourniret raped her. She was then shot to death and left in the field.

On the occasions that Olivier did not accompany Fourniret on his virgin hunting trips, she claimed that when Fourniret returned home he always told her what had taken place. He would tell her, "I went hunting" or sometimes "I obtained satisfaction".

When Olivier decided to go to the police and confess everything, Fourniret, who up until then had denied any involvement, decided to come clean. He even led the authorities to the final resting places of many of his victims. Because he was such a hated man, he had to wear a bulletproof vest on these trips in case someone decided to take him out permanently.

Investigation of Fourniret

As the investigation into the actions of Fourniret, a number of unsolved murder cases were brought into consideration as possibly being attributed to Fourniret. One of these cases was the murder of Joanna Parrish, in May 1990. A British teaching assistant who had been working in Auxerre, Burgundy, France. Joanna was kidnapped, raped and strangled to death before being disposed of in a nearby river. The similarities between her murder and many of those committed by Fourniret automatically arose suspicion.

Fourniret has always denied abducting and killing Joanna, but when his wife Olivier gave her confessions, she described a murder of an unnamed woman which was eerily similar. Joanna had apparently advertised in a magazine for English language teaching and babysitting, and Fourniret was known to read the advertisements for babysitters in the same magazine. Olivier's account of the murder included details of the injuries inflicted on the unnamed victim, and these matched the injuries found on the body of Joanna, information which had not previously been released to the media.

Olivier told the investigators how they had abducted the victim during rush hour in the evening, in Auxerre. She then drove the van towards an area of the countryside nearby while Fourniret beat the young woman until she no longer made any noise. According to Olivier, this victim, once Fourniret had finished with her, was disposed of in a 'watercourse' nearby.

However, DNA testing on semen found in Joanna's body was not a match to Fourniret, a blow that devastated her parents who had believed they finally had some sort of answer and justice for their daughter's death. But it was far from over. DNA testing was still fairly new when the testing was done in 1993, and it turned out that Fourniret's DNA was tested using a system that was incompatible with the system used to test the semen sample. In 2009, the father of Joanna, Roger Parrish, met with French investigators regarding the DNA evidence, only to be told that the evidence had been lost.

Despite denying any part in the murder of Joanna Parrish since his arrest, Fourniret finally confessed in front of a French judge on February 16, 2018, that he was the man responsible for kidnapping, raping and killing the young woman. To date further legal action against Fourniret is still being considered.

Throughout the investigation into Fourniret, spanning France, Belgium, the Netherlands, Germany and Denmark, Fourniret claimed he did not commit any rapes or murders between 1990 and 2000. However, Denmark police noticed that a police sketch of a rapist from one of their cases looked remarkably like Fourniret. Two other cases in the Netherlands showed remarkable similarities between the murders of their two victims and those of Fourniret.

One of the most interesting developments came about in 2006, regarding a highly controversial murder case from 1974. Marie-Dolores Rambla, aged just eight years old, was killed and the man believed to be responsible, Christian Ranucci, was beheaded in France by guillotine on July 28 that same year. But, as more information came to light about Fourniret's crimes, suspicions arose that perhaps it was Fourniret that was responsible, and an innocent man had been sentenced to death for a crime he did not commit.

Marie-Dolores and her brother Jean met a man in a car on June 3, 1974, who claimed he needed help to find his missing dog. Marie-Dolores got into the car to help and was abducted. An hour or so later, the car the killer had been driving was involved in an accident, but the car wasn't disabled and the man drove away. Witnesses said they saw there was a large package in the man's car, which caught the attention of the police who were searching for Marie-Dolores.

As they searched for both the young girl and the man from the accident, searchers found the body of Marie-Dolores, stabbed to death, beneath some bushes. The investigation and description of the man led police to Christian Ranucci and he was arrested. They discovered some pants in his car that had dried blood on them, and the typing of the blood was the same as Marie-Dolores. Under interrogation, Ranucci confessed and told police where he had hidden the weapon he used to kill Marie-Dolores.

There was something not right about his confession however, as he only mentioned the things that police were able to establish 48 hours after the murder. For many, it seemed the evidence was only found after he had confessed, almost as though they had been placed it there to match his confession. A day after his arrest, Ranucci recanted, saying he wasn't responsible for the murder. The blood on his pants was older than the date of the murder, and came from a motorcycle accident he had. His blood type was also the same as Marie-Dolores, and at that time, there was no way to determine whether the blood was his or hers.

The couple, who said they had seen the young girl in the back of Ranucci's car and heard her screaming, couldn't have seen him pull the girl out of the car as they originally claimed. The door was broken, and there was no way he could have opened it. Another piece of evidence was the discovery of a red sweater near the murder scene which was initially attributed to Ranucci, but later it was found he didn't own a red sweater.

Five witnesses who had seen the kidnapping of Marie-Dolores did not identify Ranucci as the offender. They all said they had seen someone who didn't match his description. Despite all of this, the killing of a young girl and the media attention it got more or less made Ranucci guilty before he even went on trial.

So why was Fourniret later considered a suspect in this case? To start with, he had gone on holiday in Marseille, where the crime occurred, in June 1974 - the same time and place as the murder.

Fourniret drove a grey car, the same color as the one seen driving off with Marie-Dolores. He also used similar ploys to get his victims into his car, and had at times used the 'lost dog' scenario. Fourniret had an extensive criminal history involving sexual deeds, particularly towards young girls, whereas Ranucci had never been arrested for anything similar.

Finally, the autopsy of Marie-Dolores showed no evidence that she had been sexually assaulted. It is known that Fourniret often ejaculates early when facing his victims and this leads to less violence towards them. So was Fourniret really the killer and not Ranucci? That question may never be answered, unless he was to confess.

Trial and Conviction

Before the trial could begin, Fourniret was assessed by psychiatrists to determine his mental state to ensure he was fit for trial. The report confirmed Fourniret was of sound, if not disturbed, mind, and therefore the trial date was set. Fourniret along with his wife Olivier went on trial on March 27, 2008, after being extradited back to France from Belgium. The charges against Fourniret included seven counts of murder, and Olivier was charged with one count of murder and four counts of complicity to murder.

Always the manipulator, Fourniret tried to dominate the court proceedings right from the beginning. He tried to prevent the media from taking photographs of him by claiming he had a right to privacy under French law. While his list of charges was read out, he sat and listened emotionless, and when the court asked him to confirm his identity, he produced a hand-written note that stated 'Lips sealed if not in closed session'. He requested that the public, the press and any photographers be removed from the courtroom, which was denied.

In response, Fourniret produced a second note and handed it to the judge. He then said, "This is the account of my acts which I intended to read," which broke his own rule of staying silent. "But I cannot talk if the court is not in camera. I ask for your permission for you to read it out yourself."

According to the note, Fourniret described himself as being "a bad being and devoid of all human sentiment". He also played down Olivier's guilt by further saying that she was "an object that my lack of morals constantly manipulated through a perverse game".

Despite his efforts, the prosecution claimed that Olivier had known all along that when Fourniret had asked her to get him a virgin, she was well aware that the victim would most likely be killed. Her lawyers attempted to show that Olivier was a weak woman who was domineered by her violent husband, and that she feared she and their son would have been killed if she didn't obey.

However, the prosecutor described Olivier as a 'deceitful witch' and a 'bloody muse' who ignored the terrified screams of their victims as her husband carried out his obscene fantasies. It didn't help her case when she admitted that they would often recreate the rape and murder scenes during intercourse with each other.

Called to testify against Fourniret were his two ex-wives and his son with Olivier, Selim. During her confession to the police, Olivier had made comments that suggested Selim had been present during some of the rapes and murders when he was a young boy. Now, he was called to testify against his own parents, which wouldn't have been easy for him.

The trial came to an end in May, 2008, after closing arguments from both sides. In a final attempt to lessen any sentence given to Fourniret, his lawyer made a plea to the jury to show compassion. He stated, "Whatever he has done, this is a man we are judging...He is part of our humanity, alas, regardless of the horrible nature of these acts."

Not surprisingly, given the confessions and evidence, Fourniret was found guilty of all charges. As the verdicts were read out, neither Fourniret nor Olivier showed any emotion. Fourniret was sentenced to life imprisonment, with the possibility of applying for parole after serving 30 years. Given his age, he would be in his late 90's by then so it is unlikely he will ever be free. Olivier was found guilty also, and was sentenced to life with the possibility of parole after serving 28 years. The court also sentenced both Fourniret and Olivier to pay moral compensation, to the value of 1.5 million euros, to the families of their victims.

At the end of the trial, Fourniret stated he would not appeal the sentence. Olivier, after the sentencing, stated that she regretted everything she had done.

Aftermath- Personal and Public

When a man such as Fourniret commits such atrocious crimes, it has far-reaching implications and effects on those who are touched by these terrible acts. It not only damages the families and friends of the victims, but also those who are close to the perpetrators. Fourniret's daughter from a previous relationship was unable to cope with fact that her father was responsible for so many murders, and two years after his arrest, she committed suicide.

There is no information on how their son Selim coped with being exposed to the rapes and murders he was made to witness as a young child. There can be no doubt that it has had some sort of long-term effect on him mentally and emotionally. Also, he was also a victim because he lost his own parents - they may be alive, but they are not free.

Because Fourniret had previously been convicted of sexual assault and rape of young girls before he embarked on his murderous spree, and that he had managed to stay under the radar throughout his crimes, the French authorities decided to come up with a method of preventing such things from happening in the future. This led to the creation of a national sex offender registry. This allowed the authorities to track sex offenders so they would always be able to determine where they were.

As a result of the errors committed by police that were unearthed during the trial, the need for better communication between the police and law enforcement authorities of both France and Belgium became clear. Both countries subsequently took a number of steps towards lessening the chance of monsters such as Fourniret from being able to prey on and murder multiple victims.

Who Was the True Monster?

A lot of the focus was on Fourniret, as the perpetrator of these awful crimes. Many thought that his partner Olivier was the meek and mild woman who was frightened to go against her husband's wishes. That she simply did what she was told to do by an overbearing and threatening husband. But was Olivier really so weak? Did she feel she had no choice, or was she just as complicit in the crimes as her husband?

Going back to her childhood, Olivier suffered with a terrible stammer, and claimed her father didn't like her because he was more interested and cared more about her brothers. As an adult,

Olivier met partner Andre in 1972, who initially hired her to work for his driving school. Before long they became a couple, and later had two sons. But, in 1982, everything changed according to Olivier. She said, "He was very jealous. One evening, while all the shutters were closed, he threw himself on me. He slapped me, tried to strangle me, it lasted for hours. He put water in the tub, pulled me into the bathroom by the mat, and plunged my head into the water, longer and longer each time. He had worked at the DST in Algeria, and said 'that's how we made Arabs talk'. The noise ended up waking one of my sons, who was one and a half years old. He came, and Andre shouted to him 'Daddy and mom are having fun, go back to bed.'"

She claimed Andre was a paranoid man, who believed that the way linen was dried hid some sort of secret code. "He was putting matches on the door to see if I was taking advantage of his sleep to go out. And then, one day, he took me by car. He stopped under the highway, near a pillar. There was a man. Andre said, 'You'll be nice to the gentleman, you'll give him a blowjob.' I went along with it because he had threatened to stop me from seeing the children."

When Olivier was being questioned in court, she was asked about her life with Fourniret. In response, Olivier stated she had always felt as though she was inferior to other people. Her life with Fourniret, in her words, was rather monotonous. She had to cook his meals using old-fashioned methods, and had to stick to recipes from the Ardennes, because that's what he preferred. When she was asked if she had ever been happy with her husband, she replied she had not.

For the trial, Olivier was assessed by psychiatrists and psychologists to try and work out her status in the relationship as far as the crimes were concerned. One expert noted that although she had no intellectual disability, she did have low self-esteem and difficulty with making decisions. Her IQ was tested at 131 by another psychiatrist who would put her in the 'gifted' range. He found that her strengths were the ability to provoke evil in men without them being aware of what she was doing. She was described as 'insensitive to the pain of others' and 'perverse'. Olivier knew absolutely that the murders were wrong, but she participated anyway.

The experts who assessed Olivier found that she was a willing and active participant in the murders and that she had no real fear of Fourniret. As one clerk described, "In the interaction between the two partners, one and the other were alternately instrument and instrumentalist."

Taking into account the psychological reports and observations of Olivier, it is hard to believe that she was the downtrodden, terrified, abused wife of Fourniret who was forced to carry out these dreadful deeds out of fear. Rather, it seems that she played a much bigger role in the abduction and murders of the young girls.

There have been several high-profile serial murder cases involving partners, most notably Fred and Rose West, and Ian Brady and Myra Hindley. In all partner cases, the woman tries to play down their part in the atrocities committed, using the excuses of being controlled by their male partner. But in every case, it is found that the women are just as involved as their counterparts. It seems that the meeting of two like-minded individuals creates the perfect setting for perverse and murderous fantasies to be carried out.

To go back to the initial question of whether or not Olivier was a monster as well as Fourniret, the evidence suggests that she indeed was just as abhorrent. She enabled her husband to carry out his fantasies by assisting with the abduction and 'medical' assessment of each victim. No matter how subservient a wife may be to her husband, no 'normal' woman would carry out such acts of perverse violence. Olivier went along with everything, and most likely played a big part in planning each crime. At no time did she report the murders to the authorities until she thought that she was going to be held legally responsible. Then she came up with the story of feeling frightened of her husband.

Latest Updates

On June 5, 2018, Olivier was back in court to discuss her husband's involvement in the murders of Joanna Parrish and Marie-Angele Domece. Both girls had disappeared and been murdered in the 1980's in Yonne. Finally, Olivier confirmed to the court that her husband, Fourniret, was responsible for the deaths.

Fourniret had denied his involvement in these two murders for years, but this year he finally admitted he was responsible. Olivier had often claimed he was involved then retracted her statements, but this time, in front of a judge, she gave the families of the victims the answers they had waited nearly 30 years for. It is now possible that a new trial will take place in 2020.

Timeline of Murder

April 4, 1942
Michel Fourniret is born.

December 11, 1987
Murder of Isabelle Laville

July 8, 1988
Murder of Fabienne Leroy

March 18, 1989
Murder of Jeanne-Marie Desramault

December 29, 1989
Murder of Elisabeth Brichet

November 21, 1990
Murder of Natacha Danais

May 16, 2000

Murder of Celine Saison

May 5, 2001

Murder of Mananya Thumphong

June 2003

Fourniret arrested

March 27, 2008

Fourniret goes on trial

May 28, 2008

Fourniret is convicted of all charges

*As the investigation is ongoing in other murders allegedly committed by Fourniret and Olivier, these cases have been omitted from the timeline.

CHAPTER 6:
Gilbert Paul Jordan - The Boozing Barber

The case of the 'Boozing Barber' is perhaps the most bizarre serial murder cases there has ever been. Jordan didn't kill his victims on the streets, and he didn't use violence to kill them. Jordan was an alcoholic and fancied the company of other addicts like himself, especially if they were women. And at that time, there were plenty of alcoholic women ripe for the picking in the local area.

What would start out as a man and woman enjoying an alcoholic beverage together would end in a dead women alone in a hotel. Then more started to turn up dead. The cause of death of all these women? Alcohol poisoning. Who were they last seen with? Jordan. This landmark case was the first of its kind, and hopefully the last.

The Beginnings of the Boozing Barber

Originally named Gilbert Paul Elsie, Jordan was born on December 12, 1931, in Vancouver, Canada. By the time he was

16, he was already an alcoholic and dropped out of high school. He ventured into a life of crime, and by the age of 21, he had been arrested for a number of unlawful acts including car theft, possession of heroin and assault.

Jordan developed a strong appetite for the combination of alcohol and sex at a rather early age. Before long he was drinking more than fifty ounces of alcohol a day, favoring vodka as his drink of choice. Like most people with drinking problems the people he associated with were typically other alcoholics. He once said that sober people didn't want to go out with him and he didn't want to drink by himself, so he drank with other alcoholics.

Later Jordan was very open about his sexual prowess, claiming to have slept with more than 200 women in a year. Whether this is true or not is unknown, but he was known to frequent the slums and dive bars in Vancouver searching for prostitutes. Therefore he may have slept with vast numbers of women, but it's highly likely they didn't choose him for his good looks and charm - instead he paid them to have sex with him.

In 1961, police pulled Jordan over and discovered a five-year-old girl in his car. She was a First Nations girl, also known as an aboriginal, and Jordan was swiftly charged with abduction. However, the case ended in May 1961 with a stay of proceedings, so he was never convicted of the crime.

Just after Christmas that same year, Jordan stood on the Lion's Gate Bridge, while intoxicated, and threatened to jump. This brought all traffic to a standstill until he finally gave up and stepped down off the railings. Not long afterwards, Jordan was in court on another matter and was charged with contempt after saluting Nazi-style at the judge.

Jordan's next major brush with the law was in 1963. He had invited two women to drink with him and lured them into his car, where he proceeded to rape them. He was arrested and charged with both theft and rape. When he went to court, he was convicted of the theft but for some unknown reason he was acquitted of the rapes. This event was just the start of what was to come, as Jordan soon progressed to committing murder.

Many Alleged Victims

Jordan's MO was to find women, usually aboriginal women, in the bars in Downtown Eastside, Vancouver, and buy them drinks. He would often pay them to have sex with him, and encouraged them to drink with him. They would drink together until the woman passed out, at which time he would then pour hard liquor down their throats.

Although several women died, the police didn't show a lot of concern. Many of the victims were known to the police as alcoholics, so it was assumed they had simply died of accidental alcohol poisoning. There were also some issues with the victims themselves, as police often didn't show as much interest in cases involving the aboriginal women, largely because many were alcoholics, drug addicts, and prostitutes.

In 1965, Jordan invited Ivy Rose Oswald, known as Doreen, to go drinking with him. Doreen wasn't like other victims, as she worked as a switchboard operator and wasn't a prostitute or known addict. The day after drinking with Jordan, her naked body was discovered in a hotel room in Vancouver, and her autopsy showed she had a high blood alcohol level. Her death was ruled an accident, but a few days after she died, Jordan applied to have his name changed from Elsie to Jordan, which was granted.

Jordan's criminal activities continued, and he raked up multiple charges and convictions for driving while under the influence of alcohol. Remarkably, in 1969, he was actually charged twice in one day for the same crime. By now his crimes had shifted from theft and drunk driving, and he had begun to be more of a sexual predator.

In 1971, he was arrested and charged for committing an indecent act in public, but the charge was subsequently dismissed. Then in 1973, he was arrested in Mackenzie and charged with indecent exposure, a charge that was upheld in court and he was convicted. In 1974, he was charged with indecent assault in Prince George, and was sentenced to spend nearly two years in prison. By 1974, the Crown had attempted to have Jordan declared a dangerous offender, but the request was denied.

Jordan was free from prison in 1975, and was back on the streets to commit more crimes. He kidnapped an unwell woman from a mental institution and was caught and charged by the police for numerous offences, including the kidnapping, and sexual intercourse with a person who was feeble minded. He received a sentence of 26 months for the assault.

Following his release from prison, Jordan opened a Barber Shop on Kingsway Avenue, after learning barbering skills while he was incarcerated. Between July 1982 and June 1985, three women died at the barber shop. Jordan had always reported the deaths after first talking to his lawyer and the coroner ruled each case was due to accidental alcohol poisoning. These victims were known to be prostitutes and alcoholics so they were considered to be at a higher risk of death by alcohol.

Suspicion fell on Jordan after the death of a woman at the Niagara Hotel in Vancouver, on October 11, 1987. Jordan had been drinking with a woman at the hotel, and on several occasions throughout the night, he made trips to the store to buy more alcohol. He left the hotel at 6am the next morning, and an anonymous phone call was made to the police at 7:40am, reporting the death of a woman at the hotel.

On arrival at the hotel, police discovered the naked body of Vanessa Lee Buckner, 27, who had sometimes worked as a prostitute but was not known to be a heavy drinker of alcohol. Her autopsy showed her blood alcohol level was 0.91, which is more than twice the amount required to kill an adult. She had also been sexually abused.

Investigation and Arrest

Police were able to track the anonymous call that was made reporting Vanessa's death. It lead directly to the room Jordan was staying in at the Marble Arch Hotel. This provided the first real link between the deaths and Jordan. Then, a month later, police were investigating the death of another woman at a different hotel, and Jordan's fingerprints were discovered at the scene. This victim, Edna Shade, had also died of alcohol poisoning. The decision was made by the authorities to begin surveillance on Jordan.

Over the next eleven days, police witnessed Jordan taking four women, on separate occasions, to various hotels in Downtown Eastside. Each time police would enter the room and put an end to the drinking binges to prevent any further victims. There was still not quite enough to prove Jordan had actually intentionally killed the other victims, so surveillance continued.

The four women police 'rescued' from Jordan were:

Rosemary Wilson - Balmoral Hotel, November 20, 1987. Her blood alcohol level was 0.52.

Verna Chartrand - Pacific Hotel, November 21, 1987. Her blood alcohol level was 0.43.

Sheila Joe - Rainbow Hotel, November 25, 1987. Her blood alcohol level wasn't measured.

Mabel Olson - Pacific Hotel, November 26, 1987. Her blood alcohol level wasn't measured.

While police were stationed outside the hotel rooms, they overheard Jordan saying a variety of things to the women, including:

"Have a drink, down the hatch baby, twenty bucks if you drink it right down...see if you're a real woman; finish that drink, finish that drink, down the hatch hurry, right down...you need another drink, I'll give you fifty bucks if you can take it..."

On the night police finally arrested Jordan, he was in yet another hotel room with a woman. On entering, they see Jordan lying on top of the unconscious victim, forcefully pouring vodka down her throat.

Conviction and Appeal

Before Jordan stood trial, he was examined and assessed by Dr. Tibor Bezeredi to determine his mental state. Dr. Bezeredi determined Jordan had an anti-social personality, defined by the doctor as "a person whose conduct is maladjusted in terms of social behavior, disregard for the rights of others which often results in unlawful activities".

Jordan was charged with first-degree murder in the death of Vanessa Lee Buckner, but the charge was eventually reduced to just manslaughter. During the trial, it was heard that Jordan had intentionally sought out up to 200 women each year to indulge in binge drinking episodes, between the years 1980 to 1988. Evidence was provided that linked Jordan to another six murders of aboriginal women, but no charge were laid.

When Vanessa Lee Buckner was killed, her blood alcohol level was more than 11 times the legal driving limit. Testimony was given at trial that Jordan had fled the hotel room and left Vanessa naked on the floor with black liquid oozing from her mouth and nose. He left her alone to die.

Jordan made a deplorable statement during his trial, stating:

"They were all on their last legs. I didn't give a damn who I was with. I mean, we're all dying sooner or later.

Jordan was found guilty of the manslaughter charge and received a sentence of 15 years. However, he filed an appeal against the sentence and it was subsequently reduced to 9 years. At the appeal Mr. Justice Sam Toy wrote, "Neither that conviction, nor any of the deaths of the preceding six victims, were alleged by the Crown to be intentional acts. Although the appellant has left a trail of seven victims, the last was the first occasion when persons in authority in a forceful and realistic manner brought to the appellant's attention the fact that supplying substantial quantities of liquor to women who were prepared to drink with him was a contributing cause of their deaths for which he might be criminally responsible."

Jordan only served 6 years of his sentence.

Other Possible Victims

Mary Johnson - November 30, 1980, Aylmer Hotel. Her Blood alcohol level was: 0.34

Barbara Paul - September 11, 1981, Glenaird Hotel. Her blood alcohol level was: 0 .41

Mary Johns - July 30, 1982, 2503 Kingsway (his barbershop). Her blood alcohol level was: 0.76

Patricia Thomas - December 15, 1984, at 2503 Kingsway (his barbershop). Her blood alcohol level was: 0.51

Patricia Andrew - June 28, 1985, at 2503 Kingsway (his barbershop). Her blood alcohol level was: 0 .79

Vera Harry - November 19, 1986, Clifton Hotel. Her blood alcohol level was: 0.04

Searching for Mary

Mary Johns' family never stopped searching for her, until she was finally found as a victim of Jordan. Although she was much loved by her family and friends, Mary lost her way after her child died from cot death. Her heart was broken at the loss of her beloved son, and to escape the pain and sorrow she fled to Vancouver.

In 1980, Mary came back home after the birth of another child, but her family said she looked much older than her years, and seemed to be worn out. It wasn't long before she disappeared again, and her family embarked on a search that lasted for six years, from 1982 until 1988, when they read in a newspaper that Mary had actually died in 1982. Tragically, just a year after the devastating news, the family was rocked by yet another death, when Mary's brother passed away from terminal cancer.

Mary's son Charlie was raised by his grandmother after his mother disappeared. He was just four years old at the time. When Charlie was 14, his grandmother passed away, and his life took a terrible turn. He began getting into trouble with the police, and went on his own search at one point trying to find his mother. He ended up living in the same Downtown Eastside of Vancouver, where his mother had last been. When Charlie was 22, he died of a drug overdose.

The whole family has endured generations of suffering, but there was still one last family member that needed to be found - Mary's last child, Billy, who vanished along with his mother. The family, who has never met Billy, believes he went into the child-care system, like so many other children of aboriginal women who either died from drug and alcohol abuse, or were murdered.

Targeting Aboriginal Women

Like numerous other serial killers, or alleged killers, Jordan knew how to choose his victims to lessen the chances of being caught. They tend to opt for those who are isolated, those that are living on the streets, the drug addicts, the prostitutes, for it is these women that are often written off as the forgotten ones, those that are less likely to be missed straight away. Jordan selected women who were predominantly aboriginal, or indigenous, and who suffered from some level of alcohol abuse. These were easy targets, and as it proved, it was much harder to pin a charge of murder on him because of the nature of the deaths - the women died while doing what they did every other day, which was consume alcohol.

In Canada, the disappearances and murders of indigenous women has been classified by many authorities as being a crisis. In homicides alone, the proportion of victims who are indigenous is extremely high compared to other nationalities. It is also more likely for an indigenous woman to go missing than any other. However, the exact number of indigenous women who had been killed or simply disappeared is not accurately known, but since the 1970s, the figure is estimated to be between 1000-4000.

Underlying factors that are believed to contribute to the higher number of indigenous female victims of violence include poverty, racism, homelessness and the legacy that stemmed from the colonialism of Canada. The residential school system that was created in Canada is also believed to be a contributing factor due to the reported abuses that occurred within the system. In 2011, a report by Statistics Canada estimated that an indigenous woman was seven times more likely than any others to be a victim of murder. Remarkably nobody had really been paying attention to what was happening in the indigenous communities, until a number of activist groups and charities got involved and pushed the government to investigate.

A Strange Method of Murder

There have been no other cases of serial murder using alcohol. The majority of killers prefer to use more violent methods, such as strangulation, gunshot or stabbing. Sometimes victims are bludgeoned to death. But nobody other than Jordan has used alcohol to kill multiple victims.

It's no wonder this case was so difficult to prosecute. After all, it was just all a bit strange. The women went with him willingly, consumed alcohol with him willingly, and if the officers outside his room that night hadn't heard Jordan urging his victim to drink more and more, he most likely would have gotten away with it.

It has to be considered that perhaps Jordan wasn't even fully aware of what he was doing. He was also intoxicated at the time of the deaths, and just maybe the women had simply drunk far too much. Almost all of the victims were known to be alcoholics or very heavy consumers of alcohol. Maybe they had just consumed one or ten drinks too many?

Then again, the circumstances surrounding each death were almost identical. It is one thing to be drinking with someone who accidentally overdoses on alcohol on one occasion. But on multiple occasions? Could someone be so unlucky as to have all these women die from alcohol poisoning in their company?

Coincidences are just that - similarities that occur at random times, in similar circumstances. But this was way too much to just be a coincidence. Was Jordan guilty of serial murder by alcohol? It seems that this is the truthful explanation between the events that took the lives of these women. In some ways, Jordan was a clever man. The idea of a serial killer using only alcohol as a weapon seemed so absurd, that there was little suspicion.

The Final Years

Jordan attempted to legally change is name to Paul Pearce in 2000, most likely as a means to start anew, without anyone knowing who he really was. At that time, a fingerprint and criminal check wasn't required if you wanted to change your name, but fortunately, that loophole was recognized and closed, and Jordan promptly canceled his application.

By 2004, Jordan was released from prison, a free man at the age of 72. But it wasn't to last; Jordan was incapable of following rules, and he violated his probation almost immediately upon his release. He was located at a hotel in Winnipeg, Manitoba, and was quickly arrested and returned to prison. Over the next two years, he was constantly in and out of prison for breaches of his parole. Then, on July 7, 2006, Jordan died of natural causes in

Victoria, British Columbia. Finally the boozing barber was no longer a problem to anyone.

Jordan's Criminal Timeline

May 1, 1961

Abduction

Police discovered a five-year-old First Nations girl in Jordan's car. Although he was charged with abduction, it ended in a stay of proceedings and he wasn't convicted.

January 5, 1963

Theft and Sexual Assault

Jordan lured two women into his car with an invitation to have some drinks with him. Police charged him with sexual assault and theft. He was convicted on the theft charge, but acquitted of the sexual assault.

April 28, 1965

First Murder Victim

Ivy Rose Oswald accompanied Jordan on one of his drinking binges. Her nude body was found in a Vancouver hotel room the next day, with a blood alcohol level of 0.51. Initially it was ruled an accidental death. A few days after her murder, Gilbert Paul Elsie applied to change his name to Gilbert Paul Jordan and was approved.

April 28, 1974

Dangerous Offender

Jordan was charged with indecent public acts and indecent assault. The Crown tried to have him declared a dangerous offender, but Jordan's lawyer intervened, and the request was denied.

April 28, 1975

Abduction

He abducted a woman from a mental institution. Police charged him on several counts, including kidnapping, and sexual intercourse with a feeble-minded person. He was sentenced to twenty-six months for assault.

April 28, 1976

Examination

Jordan was examined by Dr. Tibor Bezeredi as part of a court proceeding. Dr. Bezeredi diagnosed Jordan as having an anti-social personality, defined by Dr. Bezeredi as "a person whose conduct is maladjusted in terms of social behavior; disregard for the rights of others which often results in unlawful activities".

June 28, 1985

Death of three women

From July 1982 to June 1985, three women died as a result of alcohol poisoning at Jordan's Barber Shop. The coroner ruled all three cases to be accidental because the victims were known alcoholics and prostitutes, who were considered to be at a higher risk for such deaths.

October 11, 1987

Vanessa Lee Buckner

Jordan spent the night of October 11 drinking with a female companion by the name of Vanessa Lee Buckner at the Niagara Hotel in Vancouver. Several times, Jordan went out to buy alcohol. At six a.m. on October 12, he left the hotel for the last time. At 7:40 a.m., police received an anonymous phone call. In a room at the Niagara Hotel, they found the naked body of Vanessa Lee Buckner, 27 with a blood alcohol level of 0.91.

November 12, 1987

Edna Shade

The nude body of Edna Shade turned up at another hotel and fingerprints matched those of Gilbert Paul Jordan. Edna Shade had died of alcohol poisoning. Police placed Jordan under surveillance.

For eleven days, police watched Jordan. During that time, he took four intended victims to hotel rooms in Vancouver's Downtown Eastside. Each time, police interrupted the drinking binges.

November 23, 1987

Last Attempted Victim

Police arrested the Boozing Barber as he was poisoning his last attempted victim. She had lost consciousness. When police entered the room, Jordan was lying on top of her, forcing the contents of a large bottle of vodka down her throat.

April 28, 2004

Back on the streets

At the age of seventy-two, Jordan was once more a free man. He immediately violated his parole, and was re-arrested at a hotel in Winnipeg, Manitoba.

July 7, 2006

Death

Jordan died in Victoria, British Columbia

CHAPTER 7:
Robert Hansen - The Butcher Baker

Baker by day, butcher by night. Hansen was the pillar of his community, a well-respected businessman operating a small bakery in Alaska. He loved to hunt and fish, and enjoyed flying his small plane up to his cabin in the woods. A family man, Hansen had a wife and children, and was very much a part of their everyday lives.

But Hansen had a terrible secret life that nobody knew about. Hansen had a taste for prostitutes, but at the same time, he despised them. But they made for easy prey. The gentile baker had decided to trade in his deer he hunted for a more disturbing prey - humans. He embarked on a terrifying rampage, luring prostitutes and young women into his car, then flying them out into the wilderness where he could carry out all of his perversions. He kidnapped them, raped them, then made them run through the forest as he hunted them down.

A Troubled Start in Life

Born in 1939, in Estherville, Iowa, Hansen was the son of a Danish immigrant. Like his father, Hansen would grow up to be a baker. But as a youth he was painfully shy and suffered from a stutter, along with severe acne that left his face covered in scars. The girls at school ignored him, and this led to him developing fantasies of seeking cruel revenge upon them.

Described as a quiet loner in adolescence, Hansen hated women, and his relationship with his father was dysfunctional, due to his father's domineering behavior. He suffered from frequent bullying at school, and when he started hunting as a pastime, he found it as a source of refuge from the rest of the world.

After he left school, Hansen enlisted in the Unites States Army Reserve in 1957. He only served for a year before being discharged from the service. Later, he worked at the police academy in Pocahontas as an assistant drill instructor. It was while he was working here, that he met his first wife. They married in 1960.

Early Crimes

The same year he married, Hansen was in trouble with the law. He was arrested on December 7, 1960, for burning down the school bus garage of the Pocahontas County Board of Education. As a result, he was sentenced to three years in prison, a sentence of which he only served 20 months. However, while he was incarcerated, his wife filed for divorce. This first incarceration would be the start of what became a pattern of offending.

Hansen was jailed numerous times over the next few years, mainly for petty theft. He married again in 1963, and this marriage produced two children. The family moved to Anchorage, Alaska, in 1967, and Hansen became well-liked by his neighbors. He entered various local hunting competitions, and managed to set a number of local hunting records.

Hansen preferred the outdoors, and was well known to hunt bear, wolves and Dahl sheep, often using a bow and arrow as well as a rifle. He took up flying lessons, and eventually was able to purchase his own plane. But, before long, he was in trouble with the law again. This time it was for more than just petty theft.

In 1972, Hansen was arrested twice, both times involving crimes against women. He was charged with the abduction and rape of a woman who managed to escape him, and the rape of a local prostitute. Remarkably, he only served less than six months for these convictions. Then, in 1976, he was arrested again, this time for stealing a chain saw. He was initially sentenced to five years in prison, but this decision was overturned, as the Alaska Supreme Court felt the sentence was 'too harsh'. He would eventually only serve one year.

In 1977 Hansen was diagnosed with bipolar-affective disorder and was prescribed the drug lithium to help control his mood swings. However, he wasn't ordered to take the medication, even though he was incarcerated at the time.

After his release, in 1981, Hansen followed his father's footsteps and opened up his own bakery. Despite his troubled past, the community thought of him highly, and some described him as a pillar of the community. What they didn't know was that Hansen had financed the bakery through an insurance fraud. He had reported a burglary of his home and used the $13,000 insurance money. The fraud was investigated, and when asked how the supposedly stolen trophies had reappeared at his home, he claimed they had just turned up in his back yard and he had forgotten to notify the insurance company.

Law enforcement at the time were well aware of the smaller crimes being committed by Hansen, but they had no idea just how bad his deeds were. They could only see what was on the surface of Hansen's activities, nobody had a clue that Hansen was committing much more serious and deviant crimes right beneath their noses.

Hunting His Prey

In the 1970's, an 800-mile oil pipeline was being constructed in Alaska, and with the increase of workers came an influx of prostitutes, pimps, drug dealers and con artists. These types of people always appear when there is the possibility of separating hard workers from their income, and the construction workers involved in the pipeline were very handsomely paid. Due to the amount of money being doled out, it was common for people to leave just as suddenly as they arrived, which meant disappearances were not that uncommon.

One person, who made the connection quickly between how easy it was for people to disappear, was Hansen. Initially he had targeted women he found attractive as his victims, but he discovered that it was easier to pick up prostitutes who were less likely to be missed. So, he switched his MO and began to seek out the ladies who were working the streets at night.

Hansen would abduct his victim off the street, and transport them to remote areas outside of the city, sometimes by car, and often by plane. He would fly them out to the wilderness and force them to act out his horrendous fantasies. Sometimes they would do what he asked, and Hansen later told the authorities, "If they came across with what I wanted we'd come back to town. I'd tell them if they made any trouble for me, I had connections and would have them put in a jail for being prostitutes".

If the victim resisted Hansen's wishes, or even demanded payment for their services, they would often end up dead. The most disturbing aspect of how Hansen murdered his victims was that he would make them strip down till they were naked, then run through the forest while he stalked them. Then, once he captured them, he would slaughter them with his favorite big-game rifle or a hunting knife.

According to Hansen, his favorite place to take his victims was the Knik River valley. This area is a popular hunting ground for trophy hunters, and is only 25 miles out of Anchorage. It consists of a glacial winding gorge, making it a prime spot to hunt animals such as bears, moose, and mountain goats. It was because of this that the first discovery of human remains was made.

Two off-duty police officers from Anchorage, John Daily and Audi Holloway, were hunting along the Knik River on the afternoon of September 12, 1982, when they made an awful discovery. It was getting late in the day and darkness was descending so they decided to call it quits for the day. Both men were very familiar with the area and made their way up the river, cutting across a large sandbar, when they noticed a boot sticking out of the sand. Normally this wouldn't interest anyone, but, being police officers who are investigative by nature, they had to have a closer look.

As they got closer to the boot, they noticed it was much more than what they had initially thought. There was a partially decomposed bone joint sticking out of the sand, which shocked both men. They immediately moved away to keep the scene 'clean' and made their way back out of the gorge to their campsite, where they notified their colleagues of what they had found.

The officer assigned to investigate the case was Sergeant Rollie Port, a decorated Vietnam War veteran and considered to be one of the top investigators on the police force. He was a very meticulous investigator often spending hours going over small details and crime scenes. He arrived at the scene discovered by Daily and Holloway and supervised the uncovering of the remains. Before the body was moved, he had it photographed from every possible angle, and inspected the body carefully for any trace evidence.

Once the body was removed, Port himself began to sift the sand around the site. After several hours of careful sifting, he located a single shell casing from a .223-caliber bullet. As he was familiar with weapons, Port knew it had likely been fired from a high-powered rifle such as an AR-15 or an M-16. This was an incredibly lucky and valuable find, and those hours of meticulous searching paid off.

The autopsy of the body was undertaken in Anchorage, and the report indicated that the victim was a female, of unknown age, who had most likely been dead for up to six months. There were three gunshot wounds, the cause of death, from .223-caliber bullets. In amongst the remains had been some Ace bandages, which indicated the victim may have been blindfolded when she was killed.

Identification of the body took just over two weeks. The victim was Sherry Morrow, who had been a dancer at the Wild Cherry Bar in Anchorage. She had last been seen on November 17, 1981, and friends stated she had been going to see a man who had offered her $300 if she posed for some photographs and was never seen or heard from again.

The police were suspicious that the murder of Sherry Morrow may not have been the only murder committed. There had been a sudden increase in the number of missing persons reports filed over the past two years, and the majority of those missing were prostitutes and topless dancers. Up until the discovery of Sherry's body, not much attention had been paid to the reports as prostitutes in particular were known to move from place to place, and they often kept to themselves. Many times they simply reappeared at a later date.

The police decided to keep their suspicions to themselves, as they feared they would tip off the killer if it was made public news. When discussing the case of Sherry's murder to the news media, they stated they doubted it was related to the disappearances of other women in the area since 1980. Detective Maxine Farrell told the Daily News, "We don't believe we have a mass murderer out there, some psycho knocking off girls."

Sergeant Lyle Haugsven, an Alaska State Trooper, was given the task of determining whether Sherry's murder was an isolated incident or not. Working with the Anchorage Police Department, they began sharing files and notes between the two agencies. The first potential link related to two unsolved cases from 1980.The first case involved the discovery of partial remains of a female in a shallow grave near Eklutna Road, which had been found by construction workers. Some of the remains had been removed by animals, and there was little evidence at the burial scene.

This victim was dubbed Eklutna Annie, and to date has never

been identified. Her autopsy showed she had been stabbed to death, most likely in 1979. Later on in 1980, another victim was discovered in a gravel pit near the same location Eklutna Annie had been found. This time identification was made, and the victim was Joanne Messina, a topless dancer who was local to the area. The level of decomposition was extreme, and there was little evidence found at the scene. A task force was now formed to investigate the murders.

Hansen, still acting off the radar of the authorities, decided in 1983 that it would be easier to bring his victims home instead of flying them out to the wilderness. He planned his next attempt well, referring to it as his 'summer project' later when interviewed. His first step was to send his wife and children on a holiday to Europe so he would have the house to himself. Then, he posted advertisements in the local singles newspaper, looking for women to 'join me in finding what's around the next bend, over the next hill.'

The Escapee

Hansen's 'summer project' came well and truly unstuck on the evening of June 13, 1983. Cindy Paulson, 17, managed to escape from Hansen's clutches as he was attempting to load her into his plane. Earlier, Hansen had approached her on the street and offered her $200 to perform an oral sex act on him, but, when she entered his vehicle, he pulled out a gun and held it pointed at her as he drove to his home.

Once in the house, Hansen wasted no time in raping and sexually assaulting the teenage girl, inflicting different forms of torture on her body. At one point he decided he needed a nap, so to make sure she wouldn't run away, he chained her to a post in the basement by the neck. After he woke, he forced Cindy back into his car and drove to Merrill Field Airport.

On the way to the airport, Hansen told Cindy he was going to take her 'to his cabin', which in reality was simply a meat shack in the area of the Knik River in Matanuska Valley. The only way to get there was either by bush plane or boat. Cindy was crouched down in the back seat of the vehicle, her wrists bound with handcuffs in front of her, and while Hansen was loading the cockpit of the plane, she decided to make a run for it.

Cindy crawled out of the back seat area of the vehicle and carefully opened the door on the driver's side. Immediately she began running, and headed for Sixth Avenue. Once he realised she was gone, Hansen fled after her, but he was unable to catch up to her before she was able to get help. She flagged down a truck that was driving by and the driver, Robert Yount, stopped and let her into the truck. He later recounted how shocked he was at seeing her on the side of the road in such a disheveled state.

Yount drove Cindy to the Mush Inn nearby, and Cindy raced inside and begged the clerk to phone her boyfriend who was working at the Big Timber Motel. Meanwhile, Yount carried on his journey to his workplace and once there, he contacted the police to inform them of the handcuffed woman he had just picked up along the road. When police arrived at the Mush Inn, Cindy had already left, the clerk informing them the young girl had taken a taxi to the Big Timber Motel to see her boyfriend.

Police went to the Big Timber Motel and found Cindy alone and still handcuffed in one of the rooms. They transported her to the police headquarters when she explained what had happened. Her description of her attacker led police directly to Hansen and he was brought in for questioning. However, despite his previous criminal record, officers believed his story (and his alibi provided by his friend John Henning) that Cindy was trying to cause him trouble because she had tried to extort money from him and he had refused. Hansen was set free.

Arrest and Plea Bargain

The case of the dead girls and the attack on Cindy Paulson had gone cold, and Detective Glenn Flothe of the Alaska State Troopers needed more expert help. He got in touch with Special Agent Roy Hazelwood from the Federal Bureau of Investigation and asked if he could create a criminal psychological profile. Hazelwood agreed, and using only the information from the three bodies that had been found so far he determined the killer would be an experienced hunter, would have low self-esteem, most likely have been rejected by women often and would be compelled to keep 'souvenirs' of each murder. He also felt that the murderer may have a stutter.

Former Special Agent John Douglas, of the Mind Hunter book fame, also created a profile of the serial killer. He determined the killer would choose prostitutes and topless dancers specifically because they were generally transient people who could go unnoticed more easily. By the time Douglas was formulating his profile, Hansen had already emerged as a firm suspect, so Douglas looked closely at Hansen as a man, and his background.

Douglas noted that Hansen was quite small with heavily pockmarked skin scarred by acne, and that he had a speech impediment. He believed Hansen would have been teased and bullied as an adolescent because of these factors. This would have lowered his self-esteem which would have led him to prefer to live in isolated areas. He felt that if Hansen was indeed the killer, he was probably selecting prostitutes as his victims as a way to get revenge over the women who had rejected him in the past.

As he developed the profile further, Douglas informed investigators that if Hansen was the murderer he would most likely have souvenirs from his victims. Douglas also believed that Hansen's alibi was false, that his friends were most likely lying for him, so he urged the investigators to threaten them with criminal charges if they were discovered to be lying. The men that had given the alibi for Hansen were subsequently brought back in for questioning. The investigators utilized the suggestion by Douglas, and the men quickly confessed that they had indeed lied about Hansen's whereabouts the night Cindy Paulson was abducted.

It was during these interviews that police discovered Hansen's insurance fraud he had committed. This gave them the ammunition they needed to get an arrest warrant. They had been told that Hansen had the items he had alleged stolen hidden in his basement, so search warrants were also obtained. The more the police looked into Hansen, the more they were discovering. They found out about Hansen's cabin that was located in the same area as where the women's bodies had been dumped.

Searches of Hansen's home, vehicles and plane were undertaken on October 27, 1983. During the search a number of pieces of jewelry were found, and these were identified as having belonged to some of the missing women. They also found a variety of firearms hidden in the attic, but the biggest discovery was an aviation map hidden behind the headboard of Hansen's bed. This find was significant because of the 'x' marks that seemed to correspond with the known locations of the bodies that had been found already.

Hansen was confronted by the police with all of the evidence they had discovered in his house, but initially Hansen denied any knowledge of it or the deaths. It didn't take long for him to crack though, and at first he tried to say it was the women's fault that they were killed. After a while he gave up, and began confessing, admitting to each item of evidence as it was shown to him. He confessed to a number of attacks against women in Alaska since 1971. He claimed that his first victims were not prostitutes or topless dancers, and they were usually young, aged between 16 and 19.

The confession lasted for more than 12 hours, all of which was recorded, and by the end of it Hansen had admitted to committing a total of 17 murders. As well as those victims he had killed there were a further 40 or more women he had attacked that he had let go, in his words because he 'believed they were honestly attracted to him'. The reason he gave why the other girls were killed was because they wouldn't give in to his demands.

According to Hansen, there had been one murder that he had found most exciting, which was the killing of Paula Golding. He abducted her, raped her then tortured her in his cabin. He then opened the door of the cabin and let her run away. However, a few moments after she ran out the door, he set off after her with his rifle. He explained with great excitement how he had hunted her, even telling how she had cut her feet really badly as she ran across some rocks. After she injured her feet, she had attempted to hide under a bush, but Hansen saw her and called out to her which terrified her. She jumped out of her hiding place and starting running, but it was open ground, and Hansen shot and killed her.

He stated to the police, "It was like going after a trophy Dall sheep or a grizzly bear."

With a massive amount of evidence gathered against Hansen, he knew there was no way he would ever get off the murder charges. He discussed the situation with his defense attorney Fred Dewey, he then organized a meeting with the District Attorney, Victor Krumm. The meeting resulted in a deal being offered to Hansen. If Hansen gave a full confession, Krumm guaranteed that he would only be charged with the four cases that they were aware of, and instead of serving his time in a maximum security institution, he would instead be able to serve his sentence in a federal facility.

Although Hansen wasn't keen on the idea of having to fully confess, he agreed to the deal, realizing it was the best option for him. As soon as the deal was signed off by both parties, he began his confession, starting with a description of a typical abduction he had undertaken. The transcript in part is as follows:

"I pull out the gun - I think the standard speech was, 'Look you're a professional. You don't get excited, you know there is some risk to what you've been doing. If you do exactly what I tell you you're not going to get hurt. You're just going to count this off as a bad experience and be a little more careful next time who you are gonna proposition or go out with,' you know. I tried to act as tough as I could, to get them as scared as possible. Give that right away, even before I started talking at all. Reach over, you know, and hold that head back and put a gun in her face and get 'em to feel helpless, scared, right there I'm sure - maybe it's not the same procedure for you - you always try to get control of the situation, so some things don't start going bad maybe I've seen some cop shows on TV, I don't know, OK?"

Towards the end of Hansen's confession, investigators gave him an aerial map of the region, hoping he could point out where the bodies of his victims were. As a result he identified 15 gravesites on the map, and 12 of these were victims the investigators didn't know about. Despite being given the general location of each gravesite, it was going to be near impossible to locate each grave. So, the investigators decided to fly Hansen to each location so he could pinpoint and show them exactly where each body lay.

Aboard a military helicopter, the first place they travelled to was along the Knick River, near to where the body of Paula Goulding was found earlier. They then flew to Jim Creek, east of the Knick, and then on to Susitna, to the west. The last places they went to were Horseshoe Lake and Figure Eight Lake. At each stop along the way, Hansen showed the investigators where each gravesite was, even though the ground was now covered in heavy snow. The investigators marked a tree at each site with orange paint so they could come back and unearth the bodies. This journey resulted in the discovery of 12 gravesites.

At his trial on February 18, 1984, and as per his plea deal, Hansen pled guilty to the murders of Paula Goulding, Sherry Morrow, Joanne Messina and 'Eklutna Annie'. The following week the Superior Court Judge Ralph E. Moody handed down a sentence of 461 years plus life, with no chance of parole. Hansen was sent to the Lewisburg Federal Penitentiary in Pennsylvania.

Finding the Dead

From the gravesites Hansen had shown the investigators, they were eventually able to locate seven of the victims by May 1984. No other remains had been found at the rest of the gravesites. Those who were located were as follows:

April 24 - Sue Luna - located at the Knik River

April 24 - Malai Larsen - located at the parking area by the old Knik Bridge

April 25 - DeLynn Frey - located at Horseshoe Lake

April 26 - Teresa Watson - located at the Kenai Peninsula

April26 - Angela Feddern - located at Figure Eight Lake

April29 -Tamara Pederson - located a mile and a half away from the old Knik Bridge

May 9 - Lisa Futrell - located south of the old Knik Bridge

Details of the Known Victims

Eklutna Annie

Age: Approximately late teens to early 20s

Date found: July 21, 1980

Location: Eklutna Lake Road

Details:

Building workers discovered a shallow grave in July 1980. The body of a young woman, half eaten by animals, was found within the grave. Positive identification was impossible so the name 'Eklutna Annie' was given.

Joanne Messina

Age: 24

Date found: July 1980

Location: Near Eklutna Lake Road

Details:

Joanne was a topless dancer. Her body was discovered in a gravel pit. Her body was in a poor state of decomposition and very little evidence could be found.

Sherry Morrow

Age: 23

Date found: September 12, 1982

Location: Banks of the Knik River

Details:

Sherry's body was found in a shallow grave on the banks of the Knik River. She had been a topless dancer and had disappeared in November 1981. The autopsy showed she had been shot in the back three times, and cartridges were found near her body, suggesting she had been killed with a .223 Ruger Mini-14 hunting rifle. However, her body was fully clothed when found and there were no bullet holes in the clothing, so it is assumed she was naked when she was shot and then dressed by the killer afterward.

Paula Goulding

Age: 17

Date found: September 2, 1983

Location: Banks of the Knik River

Details:

Paula had been a topless dancer. Her body was discovered in a grave on the banks of the Knik River. She had also been shot to death and then redressed by the killer.

Malai Larsen

Age: 28

Date found: April 24, 1984

Location: Parking area near the old Knik Bridge

Details:

Few details but was a topless dancer. Her body was located with the help of Hansen.

Sue Luna

Age: 23

Date found: April 24, 1984

Location: Knik River

Details:

Killed in 1983, but the exact date is not known. Sue was taken to the Knik River, stripped, and hunted by Hansen, who shot her to death.

DeLynn Frey

Age: Unknown

Date found: April 25, 1984

Location: Horseshoe Lake

Details:

Details are sparse, but was a prostitute. Hansen admitted this murder.

Teresa Watson

Age: Unknown

Date found: April 26, 1984

Location: Kenai Peninsula

Details:

Hansen admitted this murder and helped investigators locate her remains.

Angela Feddern

Age: 24

Date found: April 26, 1984

Location: Figure Eight Lake

Details:

A known prostitute. Few details available. Hansen admitted this murder and helped investigators locate her body.

Tami (Tamara) Pederson

Age: 20

Date found: April 29, 1984

Location: A mile and a half from the old Knik Bridge

Details:

Little known, other than was a prostitute. Hansen helped investigators find her body.

Lisa Futrell

Age: 41

Date Found: May 9, 1984

Location: South of the old Knik Bridge

Details:

Few details, but a known prostitute. Hansen helped investigators locate her body.

Andrea Altiery

Age: 24
Date found: Not found
Location: Knik River

Details:

An exotic dancer. A fish necklace that had been custom made for Andrea was found amongst other 'trophies' from murders in Hansen's possession. Hansen confessed to this murder.

Megan Emerick

Age: 17
Date found: Not found
Location: Unknown

Details:

Occupation was dancer. Hansen denied this murder but was a suspect because of an 'x' on the aviation map. However, her body has not been found.

Roxanne Easland

Age: 23-25
Date found: Not found
Location: Unknown

Details:

Hansen admitted this murder but wouldn't give details about the location of the body or where the murder actually occurred. Roxanne was a prostitute.

Ceilia 'Beth' Van Zanten

Age: 17

Date found: December 25, 1971

Location: McHugh Creek Campground

Details:

Was a dancer. Hansen denied this murder but her body was located in the same spot he had marked with an 'x' on the aviation map.

Mary Thill

Age: 22

Date found: Not found

Location: Knik River

Details:

An exotic dancer. Hansen denied this murder but an 'x' on the aviation map made him a suspect.

Horseshoe Harriet

Age: Between 17 - 21

Date found: April 25, 1984

Location: Horseshoe Lake

Details:

Her body was located with the help of Hansen, but she has never been identified.

Identifying Eklutna Annie

Alaska State Troopers appealed to the public for help in identifying Eklutna Annie on February 21, 2003. Twenty years had passed since her decomposed body had been discovered and they were still no closer to finding out who she was. A reconstruction of her face had been created, but this hadn't brought any closure to the mystery.

The Troopers released further information about the mystery woman including that she had been a white woman with brunette hair. When her body was found, she was wearing reddish-brown knee high high-heeled boots, jeans, a sleeveless knit top and a brown leather jacket. Also found with her body was a silver cuff bracelet with polished stones, that could have been handmade. To date Eklutna Annie has still not been identified.

Hansen's Final Days

Hansen returned to Alaska in 1988 and was one of the first inmates incarcerated at the new Spring Creek Correctional Center in Seward. His wife and two children had initially tried to continue living in Alaska after his conviction but they were the subject of harassment for two years and eventually left. His wife also filed for divorce.

While he was incarcerated at Spring Creek Hansen was documented as being a well-behaved prisoner, and was considered to be 'low-maintenance', meaning he didn't need a lot of extra attention by the staff. For many years he worked as a barber for the other inmates.

On August 21, 2014, Hansen died at the age of 75 of natural causes. His health had been declining over recent years and he had been transferred to the prison hospital the day before his death. For the families and friends of his victims, and those who had worked on the case, there would be no tears shed for the killer. For some it had taken far too long for the world to finally be rid of Hansen.

A retired Alaska State Trooper, Glenn Flothe, who had been a part of Hansen's capture, the day that Hansen died, should only have been a day for acknowledging and remembering all of his victims and their families. He stated, "As far as Hansen is concerned, this world is better without him. It's a sad day for me, for their families."

Not only had Hansen viciously and callously murdered 17 women, he had raped at least another 30 over a period of 10 years. Frank Rothschild, the assistant district attorney who had tried Hansen's murder case, said the following:

"Good riddance to him. He's one of those kinds of guys that you kind of hope every breath he takes in his life, there's some pain associated with it, because he caused such pain."

Rothschild recalled the day prosecutors had sat down with Hansen and how he had shown the 'monster he was' when they produced the evidence they had against him. Rothschild stated about the transformation of Hansen on that day as, "He was mild-mannered Bob the Baker, and as I'm looking at him, all of a sudden he transformed. The hair on the back of his neck stood up and his neck got red, and he was pissed.

"I can still see him when he got livid like that. When Hansen left the room to speak to his attorneys, you could hear him screaming at his lawyers."

"It was just so heavy to see what this human being was capable of doing. In his mind, there were good girls and bad girls. They were all purposefully bad girls."

Hansen's Timeline of Events

1939

Born Robert Christian Hansen in Esterville, Iowa. Hansen was left handed but his parents tried to force him to be right handed. Developed a stutter.

1949

Moved back to Iowa from California. His father was a strict disciplinarian. Hansen worked in his father's bakery at a young age, earning between 35 cents and $1 a day.

1951

Attended Junior High School. Was often humiliated in school due to his stutter. Was teased by girls. Hansen hated school, and felt rejected by his classmates and inadequate.

1953

Attended High School and worked in the family business. His parents were strict and religious and there was little money. Hansen was prevented from participating in most social activities. Described as a loner. Did participate in chorus, pep club, typing and driver's ed. Played basketball. Letters in track for long distance and broad jump. Preferred solitary activities such as archery, fishing and hunting.

1957

Graduated from high school. His name was spelled incorrectly in the yearbook. Joined the Army Reserves, and attended basic training at Fort Dix in New Jersey. Had his first sexual encounter, with a prostitute in a hotel room.

1959

Returned to Iowa and worked in the bakery. Became a drill instructor for Junior Police and was in the Army Reserve Military Police.

1960

Married his first wife. Became a volunteer fireman. Set fire to the school bus garage and received a sentence of 3 years. Served only 20 months. His first wife divorced him.

1963

Met and married his second wife.

1967

Hansen and his family moved to Alaska.

1969

Had animals entered into Pope & Young's trophy hunting world record books.

1970

Had animals entered into Pope & Young's trophy hunting world record books.

1971

Had animals entered into Pope & Young's trophy hunting world record books.

1973

Megan Emerick disappears from Anchorage.

1975

Mary K. Thill disappears from Seward.

1977

Arrested and convicted of stealing a chainsaw. Given a sentence of 5 years but only served 1.

1980

Body of Eklutna Annie is found. Roxanne Easland disappears from Anchorage. Joanne Messina disappears and her body found later in the year. Lisa Futrell is last seen in Anchorage.

1981

Received money from a false insurance claim and opens his own bakery. Andrea Altiery disappears from Anchorage. Sherry Morrow also disappears from Anchorage.

1982

Bought his own plane but never got a pilot's license. Sue Luna disappears from Anchorage. Sherry Morrow's body discovered.

1983

Paula Goulding is last seen in Anchorage. Victim escapes from Hansen, he was questioned, and police accepted his alibi. Paula Goulding's body is found. Hansen brought in for questioning. House and plane searched. Evidence discovered. Charged with first-degree assault and kidnapping, five counts of misconduct in possession of a handgun, theft in the second-degree, theft by deception in insurance fraud. Further forensic evidence found and Hansen charged with four counts of first degree murder.

1984

Hansen pleads guilty to all charges. A deal is made in exchange for a full confession and assistance in finding the bodies. Hansen sentenced to 461 years plus life with no parole. Sue Luna's body found. Malai Larsen's body found. DeLynn Frey's body found. Teresa Watson's body located. Angela Feddern's body found. Tamara Pederson's body found. Lisa Futrell's body found.

1988

Returned to Alaska and incarcerated in Spring Creek Correctional Center in Seward.

1990

Second wife files for divorce and leaves Alaska due to harassment.

2014

Hansen dies of natural causes, aged 75 years.

CHAPTER 8:

Steve Wright - The Suffolk Strangler

Wright once held a respectable job aboard a luxury liner, before venturing into the business of running pubs. While he was at sea, he developed an obsession with prostitutes, visiting them at every port the ship docked in. He even continued to see prostitutes behind his wife's back, and went so far as to get into serious debt to fund his habit.

Then, women began to show up murdered close to where he lived, in Ipswich. Each of the victims had been a known drug addict and a prostitute, just the kind of women Wright liked. As each body was discovered, the community became not only terrified of this unknown killer, but also outraged. Media coverage was extreme, and as soon as a suspect was arrested, it was broadcast to every possible media outlet.

The first suspect turned out to be a red herring. But the second, Steve Wright, quickly became the number one suspect. There was a lot more to Wright than anyone ever knew. It seemed that not only did he enjoy the services of prostitutes, they satisfied him in a whole other way. For Wright had finally acted on his fantasies, and transformed from a sex addict to a serial killer.

The Early Days

In April 1958, Steve Wright was born in Erpingham, England. His father Conrad was a military policeman and his mother Patricia was a veterinary nurse. In his early childhood the family had also lived in Singapore and Malta due to his father's military service. When he was 6 years old, his mother left the family, and Wright and his three siblings stayed with their father, who eventually remarried and fathered two more children.

Wright left school in 1974 and shortly afterward joined the Merchant Navy. He worked as a chef on ferries in Felixstowe, Suffolk. By the time he was 20, he had met and married his first wife, Angela O'Donovan. The marriage produced a son, Michael, but in 1987 they separated and later divorced.

After the failure of the marriage, Wright went back to working at sea, on board the QE2 ship. It was during this time that he developed a taste for the services of prostitutes, visiting brothels at the various ports the ship docked at. His girlfriends and wives never knew about these urges Wright experienced, oblivious that he was engaging with prostitutes so frequently.

In 1987, Wright had married Diane Cassell who he had met on board the QE2. By then, Wright was a steward and Diane worked in the shop on board the ship. They hadn't been together for very long when they married, and Diane saw Wright as a charming and considerate man. However, once they moved in together in Halstead, Essex, she began to see the violent side of Wright.

A neighbor later said about their relationship, "Steve used to strangle Diane right in front of us. He would pin her up against the wall and put both hands around her throat. There were at least three times when he did it in front of witnesses. It would end when either my ex-husband or I would pull him off or he would come to his senses."

She continued to say, "He had an ability to have a violent row one minute and then have a calm conversation with you straight afterwards, as if nothing had happened. The only way I can describe it is to say he was a real Jekyll and Hyde character. He definitely had a psycho side to him."

Wright was working in the White Horse pub in Chislehurst in 1989 when he met Sarah Whiteley. They moved to Plumstead nearby and ran the Rose and Crown pub together. In 1992 the couple had a baby daughter. Described as a loving and kind father, it wasn't long before Wright began to fall into his old ways of drinking excessively and gambling. Eventually he lost not only his job at the pub, but also his wife and daughter.

Wright first attempted suicide in 1994, by gassing himself in his car. But he was quickly discovered and pulled out of the vehicle by the police. Then six years later he tried to end his life again, this time by taking an overdose of pills, but once again, his bid to die failed.

Wright was living in Felixstowe, near his father, and took on a variety of odd jobs. He had no control over his spending however, with much of his income being spent on prostitutes. At one point he was working in a fruit machine arcade, and was accused of stealing money. He then went to work in a bar at the Brook Hotel, where he was once again caught stealing money. This time he was charged, and it was the only conviction on his record.

But in 2001 he met Pamela Wright (a true coincidence that they had the same surname) and they developed a relationship. They moved in to a small flat in Ipswich, and both took on night jobs. Wright worked as a forklift driver at the docks and Patricia worked at a call center. Unfortunately his relationship with Patricia wasn't enough to quell his urges, and Wright continued to enjoy the services of prostitutes.

A Love of Prostitutes

Wright was very well known to the local prostitutes, to the point where they had begun to nickname him 'Mondeo Man' because of his car and 'Silver-backed Gorilla' because he had grey hair and a stocky build. Some of the working ladies claimed Wright liked to wear a black curly wig and dress up in tight women's clothing.

Despite the nicknames, which didn't seem to be that bad, some of the prostitutes were scared of Wright and were afraid of having sex with him. This was because of what they deemed weird behavior. Wright often drove up and down the streets looking for prostitutes while wearing PVC skirts, high heels and a wig. Other times he wore camouflage trousers, leading some to call him 'the soldier'.

One of the prostitutes that knew Wright stated, "If you didn't get in the car he would get naked and just sit there with the headlights on. He freaked me out. The police knew about him."

Wright's bill for the constant use of prostitutes was very high, so in an effort to pay for his indulgences, he bought a car worth £13,000 on hire purchase. He then sold it to fund his spending on sex, and all the while was running up massive credit card bills. Eventually, his debt reached £40,000, so Wright sold off some of his furniture then declared himself bankrupt.

Wright fled the country to Thailand, and quickly developed a relationship with a girl, Wisa Willshire. He lavished her with expensive gifts of lingerie and gold jewelry, but all the while was managing to sneak prostitutes into his hotel room. By this point, Wright no longer felt that sex was enough, that he had other urges and fantasies he wanted to explore. Wright had developed an urge to commit murder.

Crossing into Murder

On December 2, 2006, the body of a young woman was found in the water of Belstead Brook, Thorpe's Hill, near Hintlesham. A member of the public had made the discovery, and the victim was later identified as Gemma Adams, aged 25. Her autopsy revealed she had not been sexually assaulted.

Just six days later, on December 8, another body was discovered in the water at Copdock Mill near Ipswich. The victim was Tania Nicol, 19, a friend of the first victim, who had disappeared October 30. Again there was no evidence of a sexual assault.

A third body was discovered in woodland near Nacton on December 10. The victim was Anneli Alderton, 24. They autopsy showed she had been killed by asphyxiation, and had been three months pregnant at the time of her death.

On December 12, two more victims had been found. A member of the public had noticed one of the bodies lying six meters from the main road. As police conducted their investigation at the scene, a helicopter located the second body. One of the victims was Paula Clennell, 24, who had disappeared two days earlier. She had last been seen in Ipswich and had died due to compression of her throat. The second victim was identified as Annette Nicholls, 29, who had been missing since December 5.

The Victims

Gemma Adams

Gemma began using drugs as a teenager, and by the time she went missing at the age of 25, she had progressed from smoking cannabis to being hooked on heroin. As a result, she had turned to prostitution to fund her addiction, having previously been sacked from a good job she had with an insurance company because of her drug use.

She had been living in Ipswich at the time of her murder. She had disappeared on November 15, in the early hours of the morning. When her body was discovered in the river, she was naked.

Tania Nicol

Tania had gone missing on October 30, and her disappearance was officially reported to the authorities on November 1. She too had been living in Ipswich, and had developed an addiction to both cocaine and heroin. Tania worked as a prostitute to fund her habit, and at one point was working in massage parlors. However, she was dismissed from working in the parlors when it was suspected she was using drugs. She kept her lifestyle secret from her family, and it wasn't until after her death that her mother discovered Tania hadn't been working at a hair salon or bar after all.

After her body was found, the autopsy was unable to determine how Tania had been killed. What was clear was that she hadn't been sexually assaulted.

Annette Nicholls

Initially it was reported that Annette had gone missing on December 4, but it was later discovered that the last time she was seen was on December 8. Annette was a mother of one child, and was living in Ipswich at the time. She had been a drug addict for a long time, and had worked as a prostitute, just like the previous victims, as a way to fund her drug use. Her child had been taken in by Annette's mother, and when she disappeared, people thought she was living with a man.

The oldest of the victims, Annette was found on December 12, naked, and her body was left posed in the position of a crucifix. The autopsy showed she hadn't been sexually assaulted, and no definite cause of death could be established. However, the results did show that her breathing had been 'hampered' in some manner possibly leading to her death.

Anneli Alderton

Anneli was last seen on December 3, traveling to Ipswich by train. Seven days later, her naked body was discovered in a wooded area near Amberfield School in Nacton. She too had been posed in a crucifix position, and has been asphyxiated. Anneli was a 24 year old mother of a five year old son, and was in the early stages of pregnancy when she was murdered. Her life had taken a terrible turn in 1998 following the death of her beloved father, which led her to a life of drug and alcohol abuse and prostitution. At the time of her death, she was living in temporary accommodation, with no fixed abode.

Paula Clennell

A mother of three, 24 year old Paula went missing on December 10 in Ipswich. Her naked body was found two days later, and the autopsy reported she hadn't been sexually assaulted and had been killed by compression of her throat, cutting off her airway. Paula had become addicted to drugs, and like so many others, was working as a prostitute to fund her habit. All of her children had been taken away and placed into care due to her lifestyle.

Ironically, shortly before her disappearance Paula had given an interview to Anglia News regarding the murders of the other prostitutes. She had stated that although the murders had made her "a bit wary about getting into cars", she continued to work as a prostitute because "I need the money".

Operation Sumac

It didn't take long for the Suffolk police to link these murders together, and an investigation was launched with the codename 'Operation Sumac'. On December 10, a press conference was held where the detectives issue a warning to all of the women in Ipswich, that they should not work on the streets. It was also announced that some of the neighboring police forces had offered their assistance in the hunt for whoever was responsible for the murders.

Due to the size of the investigation, Chief Constable Alastair McWhirter stated they would have to be reliant on external forms of assistance. The day-to-day investigation was headed by Detective Chief Superintendent Stewart Gull, and Commander Dave Johnston from Scotland Yard was brought in as an advisor.

Further press conferences took place on December 13, and

December 14, and Gull acknowledged that they believed the locations of the bodies found were not the actual murder sites, but instead they were dump sites. They did not know however, where each victim was actually murdered, whether they had all been killed in one place or at multiple locations. Some items belonging to the women had been discovered, including clothing and a handbag, and these were being scientifically examined. By this time, there were more than 200 police officers brought in to the investigation, and up to 450 calls were being received daily with potential information.

By December 15, 7,300 phone calls had been made to the police about the investigation. There were 26 extra police forces now assisting the Suffolk police with the case, and the number of officers now working the investigation had reached 250. That number had increased to 500 within a few days, and another 350 officers from other police forces were assisting. One of the most tedious aspects of the investigation involved watching more than 10,000 hours of CCTV footage to try and find evidence of the women who were murdered and who they may have been with when they disappeared.

The investigation also included searches of 176 sites around Ipswich, and approximately 1,500 door-to-door enquiries. Police conducted interviews with other prostitutes in the town to glean information about their clients, and if there were any that set off alarm bells with any of the women. During the investigation, several men had drawn the attention of police, and one man in particular stood out above the rest.

Tom Stephens had contacted police after the disappearance of Tania Nicol, and he made several other calls regarding the case over the weeks of the investigation. Police placed him under surveillance, and on December 18 he was arrested and questioned about the five murders.

In the meantime, DNA evidence was being analyzed. The killer had become careless, and after dumping the first two victims in water to obscure any evidence, the last three were dumped in the woods, and DNA was recovered from each body. On December 17, police were notified that there had been a breakthrough in the DNA analysis, and a suspect was identified. It was Steve Wright, whose DNA was added into the national crime database after he was convicted of theft in 2002.

Wright was placed under surveillance and arrested on December 19. He was interviewed by police, at length, and finally was charged with all five murders. The initial suspect, Tom Stephens, was released and determined to be innocent of the crimes.

The Jury Decides

On December 22, 2006, Wright appeared before the magistrates in court to answer the charges, and he was subsequently remanded in custody to await his trial. The trial date was set for

January 16, 2008. The first jury selection consisted of 10 men and 2 women, but they were stood down due to the illness of one of the potential jurors, and another jury selection took place. The second jury consisted of 9 men and 3 women. As part of the selection process, all jurors had to complete a questionnaire, stating that they didn't know any of the witnesses, the victims, or the suspect.

Wright's defence lawyer, Timothy Langdale QC, commented that it was difficult for the jurors to state they knew nothing of the case due to the massive amount of information that had been given in the media. Therefore, the judge instructed the jurors to only consider what information and evidence was given during the trial, and to ignore anything else they may have heard or read prior to their selection as jury members.

The prosecution was quick to bring to the jury's attention the amount of DNA and fiber evidence linking Wright to the murders. The defence responded by arguing that Wright was known to frequently engage the services of prostitutes and he had indeed had sex with all of the victims except for Tania Nicol. Wright stated he had picked Tania up one night but had changed his mind about having sexual intercourse with her and dropped her back off in the red light district in Ipswich.

However, Wright had been stopped by police in that same area in the early hours of the morning and he had claimed that he didn't know what district he was in, and that he had no idea it was where prostitutes could be found. He further explained to the police officers that he was simply driving around because he couldn't sleep.

During the trial, the jury was taken on excursions to visit the sites that were relevant to the case. This included the location of Wright's rented home, and the five sites were the bodies had been discovered. It was noted by the prosecution that Anneli Alderton's body was found quite a distance from the road, but there was no evidence discovered that showed she had been dragged there by one man. This inferred there may have been an accomplice, but there was no real evidence to suggest this was true.

At the end of the trial, the judge summed up to the jury as follows:

"The loss of these five young lives is clearly a tragedy. You are likely to have sympathy for the deceased and their families. Your sympathy ... must not sway you ... You may view with some distaste the lifestyles of those involved ... whatever the drugs they took, whatever the work they did, no-one is entitled to do these women any harm, let alone kill them."

It took just eight hours for the jury to reach a decision. On February 21, they announced they had unanimously decided on the verdict on all five murder charges. They found Wright guilty. A conviction for murder carries an automatic life sentence but the judge would be required to decide if there should be any eligibility for parole. Not surprisingly, the judge sentenced Wright to life imprisonment without parole. He reached this decision due to the amount of premeditation and planning Wright had displayed in committing the murders.

Although Wright was to be sent to prison for the rest of his natural life with no chance of being released, for some family members of the victims it wasn't enough. Some felt that Wright should have been given the death penalty. One such family member, Craig Bradshaw who was the brother-on-law of Paula Clennell, stated, ""Today, as this case has come to an end, we would like to say justice has been done but we're afraid that where five young lives have been cruelly ended the person responsible will be kept warm, nourished and protected. In no way has justice been done. These crimes deserve the ultimate punishment and that can only mean one thing. Where a daughter and the other victims were given no human rights by the monster, his will be guarded by the establishment at great cost to the taxpayers of this country and emotionally to the bereaved families."

For the father of Gemma Adams, the reaction was different. After the verdict he said, "I am very relieved and pleased for all of the families that this is now over and we can now start to get on with our lives."

Wright subsequently lodged appeals against his convictions and the sentence imposed following his trial. In one case he claimed the trial should have been held elsewhere instead of Ipswich, and that the evidence presented against him was not enough to prove he was guilty.

While he was in prison awaiting his trial, a letter he wrote to his father gave a small glimpse into his mind and the possible reason why he killed these women. In the letter he wrote, "Whenever I get upset I tend to bury it deep inside, which I suppose is not a healthy thing to do because the more I do that the more withdrawn I become because I have seen too much anger and violence in my childhood to last anyone a lifetime."

The true motive for the murders may never be uncovered, but according to consultant psychologist Dr. Glenn Wilson, the motive was most likely sexual. He also believed Wright killed the women by strangulation as a way to satisfy a fetish. Throughout Wright's life, there had been themes of violence, sexual deviance and addictive behavior, which all contributed to his somewhat chaotic way of life.

Wright was almost a clever killer, trying to make sure he left no evidence behind at the scene of each body that could be linked back to him. He made sure to wear gloves, and always cleaned his car thoroughly after transporting each body to the dump site. But, he had obviously forgotten that he had previously been forced to supply a DNA sample after he was arrested years earlier.

Possible Links to Other Murders

There are a few cases of murdered women that police investigators still consider Wright to be a suspect in. One of these cases was the murder of Suzy Lamplugh, who was last seen alive in 1986. She had worked with Wright on board the QE2 ship in the early 1980s. She was working on the ship as a beautician, and was known to be an acquaintance of Wright. Her body has never been found, and she was officially declared deceased in 1994.

It was reported that after Wright moved to Brixton, Suzy Lamplugh would often go and visit him. At the time of her disappearance, Wright's ex-wife claimed he was on shore leave, and not on board the ship.

Although the Suffolk police would neither confirm nor deny they had considered Wright to be a suspect in the disappearance of Suzy, it is known that Scotland Yard had made contact with them regarding the case following the conviction of Wright for the other murders.

Wright was at one point considered to be a person of interest in the murder of heroin addict Vicky Glass. She had disappeared from Middlesbrough in September 2000, and her naked body was later found in a stream on the North Yorks Moors. Cleveland Police subsequently ruled out a link between this murder and Wright.

The third case where Wright has come under scrutiny is the murder of Michelle Bettles. This was first considered a possible link to Wright through criminologist David Wilson, due to the nature of the disappearance and the murder itself. Michelle, 22, was a prostitute who was last seen alive in the red light district of Norwich on Easter Weekend, March 2002. She was meant to be meeting up with a regular client, but CCTV footage showed her going in the opposite direction from the prearranged meeting place.

Her body was discovered on the morning of March 31, 2002, in a wooded area by a country track known as Rush Meadow Road, Scarning, near Dereham. This site is around 20 miles away from where she had last been seen. Michelle had been strangled to death.

Despite the similarities between Michelle's murder and the other murders committed by Wright, the police did not consider Wright to be a suspect in the killing. To date, the case is still open.

Controversial Media Coverage

At the beginning of the investigation, a local company, Call Connection, put up a £25,000 reward, which they ended up raising to £50,000. Then, the News of the World offered a huge reward in addition, of £250,000 for any information leading to an arrest and conviction of the murderer. By now the press had likened the killer to another serial killer, Peter Sutcliffe, the 'Yorkshire Ripper', and as is typical with media, they soon developed the name 'the Suffolk Strangler' when discussing the five murders.

Immediately after the two initial suspects were arrested, the Attorney General Lord Goldsmith issued guidelines to the media about their coverage, following concerns raised by the Suffolk police that information portrayed in the media may hinder any trial and conviction results in the future.

Michael Crimp, who was a senior prosecutor on the case, was also concerned about potential prejudice due to what was printed in the media. He said, "Steven Wright stands accused of these offences and has a right to a fair trial before a jury. It is extremely important that there should be responsible media reporting which should not prejudice the due process of law."

As well as the outrage created by the horrendous nature of the crimes, this case also had a major impact on several serious issues that were facing the United Kingdom at that time. Firstly, it highlighted just how dangerous a lifestyle prostitution was, and how vulnerable the ladies were who worked the streets at night. It brought forward calls to the government to either impose more fines and convictions against prostitutes, or to change legislation so that they could work in a legal brothel setting. The general aim was to improve the safety of those women who either wanted or were forced to work as prostitutes. As a result, the government strengthened its anti-prostitution laws and focused the attention on the 'clients', those who used the prostitutes rather than the women themselves.

The idea of 'mini brothels' was pondered at one point, but this concept was abandoned due to fears that it may encourage drug dealers and pimps to shift into the area and thus bring further trouble. So, the Policing and Crime Act 2009 was enacted which made it illegal to pay for the services of a prostitute who had been 'subjected to force'. This also applied to clients who were unaware that the woman was being forced to work as a prostitute.

The second major impact on the legal system and government concerned the legality of illegality of using drugs. There were calls for drug addicts to receive their drugs on prescription, to stop them from purchasing on the street. Some felt that illicit drugs should be decriminalized, to both stop the street buying and also to remove the stigma associated with drug addicted prostitutes. Research at the time showed that up to 95% of prostitutes working in the UK at the time were addicted to drugs and or alcohol.

There were media issues surrounding the identification of the first suspect Tom Stephens. The police had never formally released his name, but the media were quick to broadcast his identity once they were aware of whom he was. Stephens had given interviews to both the Daily Mirror newspaper and the BBC, and these were released to the public before he was arrested, which would have severely hampered any potential trial in the future, should he have been charged.

Overall, cases such as this one will always draw intense media and public scrutiny, but it is how the information is handled and released which causes the most severe damage. Ultimately, any suspect or arrested person has the right to a fair trial in court, and this is not always possible in this day and age because of the power of the media. Where once details may be reported in the daily paper or broadcast on the radio and television news, nowadays it appears everywhere thanks to the internet. Different media outlets race to publish every little juicy tidbit, often digging up historical information about the suspect, which can definitely color the perception of the person and the crime by the jury.

Unfortunately it is near impossible to stop the media from releasing information. While an authority may try and legally obtain a media ban, there is always going to be someone who gives out details through the internet. We are all guilty of developing a perception of a person based on information we are given, and the onus is ultimately on the jurors to be able to put aside what they know and focus on what they are given in the courtroom.

Where did it All Go So Wrong?

A documentary called 'My Son the Serial Killer' delved into the thoughts and opinions of Wright's father, Conrad, and experts on what they believed led to Wright committing five atrocious murders. Conrad commented that he thought it all went back to the day Wright's mother left the family along with his sisters. On that day, Wright watched them leave from an Ipswich train station, and it was the last time he ever saw his mother. One of the experts in the documentary said that this abandonment in childhood by his mother indeed set in motion what would later become of Wright.

At the time his mother left, Conrad said that they had 'sort of' agreed to a break from each other, but that he never thought she would actually leave for good. Wright was just eight years old the last time he saw his mother. It's important to note, that although this abandonment may have had a direct impact on Wright as he became a man, it couldn't be the main blame for his actions.

Dr. Elizabeth Yardly stated in the documentary, 'I think that Wright's upbringing did play a part in what he became. I think it started to write the script for what he would become. But I think we have to be careful when we're looking at people's backgrounds, because lots of people have disrupted childhoods, lots of people have parents who separate - very few of them are going to go on to harm anybody else.'

Conrad claimed he had never suspected his son was capable of committing murder, and he finds it very difficult to accept Wright took the lives of five women. He also stated that he would never forgive his son for what he did to the victims and their families.

Some experts don't believe Wright only started killing women once he was aged in his 40's and that there were most likely other victims prior to the ones that are known about.

To this day, Wright has never confessed to killing the five victims. He did admit to having sex with four of the women, but denies ending their lives.

The Lucky Ones

Following Wright's arrest and convictions, more stories appeared of those who had come into contact with Wright and lived to tell the tale. One of these lucky women was former prostitute Lindi St. Clair, from Herefordshire. She had endured a terrifying experience back in the 1980s, and once she saw Wright's photograph in the media after he was arrested and charged, she finally knew who the man was who had attacked her all those years ago.

According to St. Clair, Wright had gone to visit her for a 'regular service', and when he had finished, he suddenly lunged at her with his arms stretched out trying to grab her throat. As he did so, he said "I know you, I know you."

St. Clair managed to jump out of his reach and escaped out the door and into the street to save herself. Now, years later, she made a formal report to the police about the incident, because now she could tell him who her attacker was.

She had always taken extra precautions while working as a prostitute to try and keep herself safe. Whenever she met a client, she made sure she had an escape route planned, and she carried alarms to frighten off any would-be attacker.

Some may think it's convenient that she was able to recognize Wright from his photograph, and that maybe she could be mistaken. But as she said, "I recognized the photograph and when you are attacked by somebody you take an instant snapshot in your head of the face."

Another former prostitute who was lucky enough to not become one of Wright's victims was Jade Reynolds. The very first time she went out on the street to work as a prostitute, the first client she had was Wright. She had been a heroin addict, and turned to prostitution to pay for her drug habit.

When she first met Wright, she was standing on a street corner in the red light district of Ipswich when he approached her. They agreed on a price for sex and went to a spot near the riverside. According to Jade, he was never aggressive or rude to her, and was just like any other client she had. It wasn't until his arrest was made public eight years later that she realized how lucky she had been.

"I couldn't quite believe it. I hadn't really thought any more about it, to be honest. He wasn't a regular of mine or anything. I think I went with him about six times in all."

Tracy Russell had also been hired as a prostitute by Wright for around three years, on and off. When she discovered she had been hired after he had killed his fifth victim, she was stunned. Right up until that night, her experiences with Wright had always been normal. He always turned up nicely dressed and clean, but on this night everything about him was different.

He picked her up and took her back to his house he shared with Pam, his girlfriend, who wasn't home at the time. This night he was unkempt, dirty and sweaty, and his behavior was more aggressive and what she described as nasty.

Wright pinned her down, which was something he hadn't done to her before. She was scared, as it wasn't the way Wright usually was with her. He said to her, "I don't want to rush tonight. I will pay you extra. I will pay you £100."

Suddenly there was a 'bang' noise and he told her to quickly get out. He wanted her out of the house so fast he was trying to help her get dressed to speed it up. Then he made her go out the front door, which was weird to Tracy.

Later, when she found out about his arrest, she realized that whatever that loud noise was that night that frightened Wright, it possibly saved her life.

Did He Work Alone?

There has been much debate about whether or not Wright had an accomplice. During his trial, both the defense and the prosecution mentioned that Wright may have been assisted by somebody when he killed the five prostitutes. And there are a number of reasons why this has been considered a possibility.

On the night Tania Nicol disappeared, a witness had seen her talking to the driver of a vehicle, and they were certain there were two persons in the vehicle not just one. There was also the mystery about how the body of Anneli Alderton had been carried to where she was finally found. There was no evidence of her body having been dragged, no marks on the ground or in the foliage, which suggested she had been carried there by two people.

Another important witness statement relates to the vehicle owned and driven by the original suspect Tom Stephens. The night Annette Nicholls disappeared, Stephens' car was seen parked near Wright's vehicle close to where her body and the body of Paula Clennell were found.

Despite the allegations and suggestions, Stephens denies having anything to do with Wright or the murders. According to him, the only reason he was initially questioned and arrested was because he made a phone call to the police stating that he thought he may have a split personality, and that he could have been doing things which 'he doesn't know about'.

However, Stephens did admit that he had had sex with all five victims. And while he was being questioned, he told the investigators that if he had been the murderer, he would have strangled the victims. Another important piece of information was that his alibis for the nights the women disappeared could not be established.

But, when police searched his flat, they found no evidence to suggest he may have been involved in the murders. Witness statements, along with one from a former prostitute who claimed Stephens had once pinned her down during sex, were not enough to build a case against Stephens. Investigators said that Stephens was interviewed intensely over a four day period, and the ensuing investigation eliminated him as a suspect.

Where is He Now?

The last reported whereabouts of Wright were at HMS Long Lartin, a category A men's prison located in South Littleton, Worcestershire. It is also home to other notorious killers such as Jeremy Bamber, who killed his family, and Charles Salvador (aka Charles Bronson).

Wright has launched appeals against his convictions, the first in July 2008 which was rejected, and the second in February 2009, also rejected. In December 2016, he created fury among the families of his victims by launching yet another appeal to have his convictions overturned. His brother David is his strongest supporter, and visits him regularly in prison.

Wright's Timeline

1958

Steve Wright is born.

1978

Wright marries Angela O'Donovan.

1980's

Wright starts using prostitutes.

2001

Wright convicted of theft and his DNA added to the national database in the UK.

September 2006

Wright moves to Ipswich with his partner, into a home located in the red light area.

November 1, 2006

Tania Nicol is reported missing.

November 15, 2006

Gemma Adams is reported missing by her boyfriend.

December 2, 2006

Gemma Adams' body is discovered.

December 4, 2006

The murder inquiry is launched.

December 8, 2006

Tania Nicol's' body is found.

December 10, 2006

Anneli Alderton's body is found in woods at Nacton.

December 12, 2006

Two bodies are found, later identified as Paula Clennell and Annette Nicholl.

December 16, 2006

Confirmation given that Anneli Alderton was three months pregnant when she was killed.

December 19, 2006

Steve Wright is arrested.

December 21, 2006

Wright is charged with all five murders.

February 21, 2008

Steve Wright is found guilty of all charges. He was sentenced to life imprisonment.

More books by Jack Rosewood

From rampage killers to hunters that seek out human prey in the shadows of the night, this serial killer anthology is a collection of horror stories. Collectively these men were responsible for hundreds of deaths, and they all belong in the realm of the worst serial killers to date. Delve into eight different cases and explore the heinous deeds committed, the background of each killer, and the apparent motives for their crimes.

There are those who went on deadly rampages, such as Cho Seung-Hui and George Hennard; men who decided to inflict as much terror in one day as they possibly could. Famous serial killers are included, such as the Hillside Stranglers, Kenneth Bianchi and Angelo Buono, and the Beast of the Ukraine, Anatoly Onoprienko. There are also lesser known murderers such as Fritz Haarmann and Ronald Dominique, who preyed on young men for their own deviant pleasures.

Each of these true murder stories will leave you with a sense of horror and perhaps a little fear. David Parker Ray's surviving victims still live in fear today, and this notorious true crime story is one of the most sadistic and disturbing. With tales of torture, mind control and violence, very few survived their time in Ray's toy box.

The true crime stories in this book have been selected because of the horrendous nature of their actions and the sheer volume of victims they slaughtered. Innocent people, going about their daily business or asleep in their beds, all make up these serial killers true crime stories.

Few serial killers in history have garnered as much attention as Jeffrey Lionel Dahmer. Although Dahmer killed seventeen young men and boys, it was not so much the number of people he killed that makes him stand out among famous serial killers, but more so the acts of depravity that he committed on the corpses of his victims. In this true crime story you will read how Dahmer transitioned from a loner to serial killer, committing numerous unnatural acts along the way such as necrophilia and cannibalism. Following in the macabre tradition of another infamous Wisconsin serial killer—Ed Gein—Jeffrey Dahmer terrorized Milwaukee for most of the 1980s until he was finally captured in 1991.

Perhaps one of the most frightening aspects of Jeffrey Dahmer's serial killer career was how easy he was able to lure his victims into his trap. Dahmer possessed above average intellect, was conventionally good looking, and usually had a calm demeanor that could disarm even the most paranoid of people. Because of these traits, Dahmer was able to evade justice numerous times, which allowed him to keep killing. Truly, Dahmer was able to fool his family, the police, his neighbors, and even the judicial system into believing that he was not a threat; but during the entire time his kill count increased and the body parts of his victims began to pile up around his apartment.

Open the pages of this book to read a story that is among the most disturbing of all true crime serial killers. You will follow the course of Dahmer's life from an alcoholic outcast in high school to a vicious predator who stalked the streets of Milwaukee. Finally, you will read about Dahmer's trial, his jail house murder, and the impact that his many crimes had on Milwaukee.

→CLICK HERE←

TO SEE ALL BOOKS BY JACK ROSEWOOD

GET THESE BOOKS FOR FREE

Go to www.jackrosewood.com/free

and get these E-Books for free!

A Note From The Author

Hello, this is Jack Rosewood. Thank you for reading this book. I hope you enjoyed the read. If you did, I'd appreciate if you would take a few moments to **post a review on Amazon.**

I would also love if you'd sign up to my newsletter to receive updates on new releases, promotions and a FREE copy of my Herbert Mullin E-Book, visit www.JackRosewood.com.

Thanks again for reading this book, make sure to follow me on Facebook.

Best Regards

Jack Rosewood

Made in the USA
Middletown, DE
29 October 2020